FROM SEX SHOPS TO SUP

How adult toys became a multi-bi

By Dale Bradford

Dedicated to Lee, Lesley, Jacinta, Kirsty, Tom, Paul, and Jonny, who shared the journey with me. And to Jo, Naomi, Lauren, Ronnie, and Tabs for their support.

About the author

Dale Bradford has been editing B2B magazines since 1995. From 2003 to 2022 he was editor of *Erotic Trade Only* (ETO), the only UK-based trade publication aimed at retailers of adult toys and pleasure products.

About this book

The 21st century has seen the adult toys sector transform from being the subject of cheap jokes into a multi-billion-pound industry. It's been a fascinating journey, and thanks to my job, I had a seat up front with the driver. Actually, make that drivers, because there was more than one of them, and in this book I'll explain the part they all played and demonstrate how they fed off each other.

Adult toys – also known as 'sex toys' and the more upmarket 'pleasure products' – might not be mainstream commodities in the UK but a variety of retailers now include them in their portfolio. Shoppers can find them jostling for space with pain relief in pharmacy chains such as Boots, rubbing shoulders with upmarket beauty brands in Selfridges, and positioned a bit too close for comfort to boxes of Quality Street in Poundland (as part of its 2022 Valentine's Day displays – even I was shocked at that).

We're not quite at the stage where the Office for National Statistics adds a rabbit vibe and a water-based lube to the typical basket of goods it uses to work out the UK inflation rate, but almost every major supermarket now offers customers the opportunity to surreptitiously stick something sexy for the weekend in their trolly.

It might have taken until March 2021 for a sex toy brand to take out a full-page ad in a broadsheet newspaper (Hot Octopuss in *The Guardian*) but your nan's *Good Housekeeping* magazine has been putting vibes in the hands of its testers since 2003. And in recent years television viewers have been taken behind the scenes at pleasure product purveyors ranging in size from a family-run shop in Brighton to an industry giant with a global presence and a turnover in nine figures.

Also helping to normalise sex toys with their endorsements have been an array of celebs, from Motörhead and Mötley Crüe to Lily Allen, and who can forget when Fifty Shades Fever swept the world? Talking of pandemics, the first COVID-19 lockdown in March 2020 was reportedly responsible for a massive boost in sex toy sales, and since then the industry has seen the formation of 'supergroups' – where venture capitalists acquire several companies and bolt them together to make them even more profitable.

Depending on which Google result you click on, 'experts' are forecasting that the global market for sex toys could be worth up to $50bn by 2028, but how did we get here? By a rather circuitous route, and our starting point is the year 2000…

Contents

A IS FOR ANN SUMMERS

"Well this isn't going to work, is it? Women aren't even interested in sex!"

As television viewers watched Prime Minister Tony Blair join hands with a less-than-enthusiastic Queen Elizabeth II to welcome in the new millennium, in a cavernous tent that would eventually become known as the O2 Arena, anyone thinking of purchasing a sex toy at that moment – unlikely though it may sound, given the above mental image – would probably be planning to buy it from Ann Summers.

Although it wasn't the only game in town, it was the only game in most towns, with prominent high street locations up and down the country and an army of direct sales agents only too willing to set up their suitcases of samples in your lounge if you just invite a few chums around for the evening.

By the year 2000, Ann Summers had been trading for almost three decades under the ownership of Ralph and David Gold. The brothers had acquired the business in 1972 when it had four stores, and it became a household name after David's daughter, Jacqueline Gold, joined the firm in 1981.

It was Jacqueline's idea to supplement high street sales by introducing a party plan operation. The official line was that party plan offered women the opportunity to run their own business, achieve financial independence, and provide a safe, fun environment for them to shop for sexy lingerie and toys. Which is all very commendable. Less altruistically, it also gave Ann Summers a whole new route to market.

Inspired by the wholesome Tupperware parties of the 1970s, an Ann Summers party was a women-only event held in a consumer's house. Run by a local organiser, it took some of the fun elements of a typical hen night – including wine and saucy games to break the ice – and allowed guests to see, hear, and touch a sex toy and learn about what it could do.

Obviously the idea was to get them to buy products though, and the party hosts were rewarded with incentives such as discounts on any items they fancied from the catalogue. Participants were encouraged to host parties of their own by the organiser, who was paid a commission on sales. Those with an aptitude for the job could earn a decent salary, and the most successful qualified for a company car.

As well as introducing many women to a sex toy for the first time, the 'Ann Summers Party' has become a part of British culture. So much so that in 2016 ITV created a six-part dramady about it called *Brief Encounters*.

Based on Jacqueline Gold's 1995 memoir, *Good Vibrations: The True Story of Ann Summers*, Gold said at the press launch of the series: "The start of Ann Summers Party Plan was one of the most exciting times of my career and I have many fond memories of the women who started on this journey with me. In the early 1980s, these women were trailblazers and helped to create the opportunity for so many more women to run their own business. Since launching Party Plan, the model has given financial independence to in excess of 350,000 women, something I'm incredibly proud of."

As the *Brief Encounters* opening sequence began, to the synthpop accompaniment of The Human League's 'Love Action', we learn that it's September 1982, a pivotal period in British history. Margaret Thatcher had started the year as the most unpopular prime minister in living memory, as the unemployment total reached an astonishing three million, but by this time – despite factories continuing to close – she was riding on the crest of a wave of rediscovered patriotism, following the conclusion of the Falklands conflict a few months' earlier.

The *Brief Encounters* title appeared in the same font as Ann Summers used back then, as we witnessed a smoking woman typing up a 'wanted' ad which she intended sending to *The Sheffield Post*. The ad read: 'Ann Summers demonstrators required to run parties selling exotic lingerie. For ladies only. Earn £30-£40 per evening, Meeting Wednesday 8th September Maythorpe Community Centre 12pm'.

In those pre-internet days, small businesses were almost totally reliant on ads in local newspapers to communicate, and because they were frequently charged by the word, they became skilled in brevity. Examples on the page surrounding the Ann Summers ad included 'Fitted bedroom furniture specialists Tel: 0742 4962230' and 'Sales Supermarket req Deliver Driver. References required. 496 1112'.

I'm sure they were mocked up for the series but back in 1982 the area code for Sheffield was indeed 0742 (it changed to 0114 in 1995). It was a nice detail that only those who paused their TV picture and moved their face to within inches of the screen would ever see.

The exterior shots looked depressingly grim and the interiors featured 1970s' tones such as orange and brown – this was pleasingly authentic as decades do tend to overlap and bleed into each other rather than suddenly morphing into a new colour palette.

Our protagonists were introduced early: two cash-strapped women with children (Steph and Nita), a gum-chewing teen (Dawn), and a middle-aged pillar of the community (Pauline) who was married to a butcher. The cast was high calibre, particularly Pauline, who was played by Dame Penelope Wilton, perhaps best known as Mrs Crawley in *Downton Abbey*, though she was also Harriet Jones in *Doctor Who* and had appeared in movies as diverse as *Clockwise*, *Shaun of the Dead*, *Pride & Prejudice*, and *The Best Exotic Marigold Hotel*.

It emerged that Pauline was bored. Despite having an upmarket house with lots of mod cons and a cleaner (Steph), she felt her life had no purpose. Alone in her funereally dark wood kitchen, she ripped a pattern for a macramé owl out of a magazine. This was another nice period touch: macramé was a popular method of crafting wall hangings and decorations around this time.

As for Steph, her cleaner, we saw her telling her husband that with their son in school, she would like a more fulfilling job, and she presented him with the Ann Summers ad. But he didn't want her selling exotic underwear, despite having been laid off from the factory earlier in the day. It veered towards *The Full Monty* territory here, which was also set in Sheffield, as she retrieved the ad from the bin after he stormed out to the pub.

Next day Steph told her mum (played by Felicity Montagu, who you'll remember as Alan Partridge's downtrodden personal assistant, Lynn) that she wants to get a job in sales. "Don't be daft," her mother replies. "You've got to have something about you to do that."

Regardless, Steph and Nita attend the Ann Summers presentation at Maythorpe Community Centre, where the speaker says: "There are people out there who think women aren't interested in sex, but they're wrong and I want you to help me prove it."

This sets in motion a sequence of events too convoluted to describe here but the script – by *Smack The Pony* and *Green Wing's* Fay Rusling and Orianne Messina – flowed beautifully, with some neat one-liners. And while it wasn't exactly family viewing (the subsequent DVD release was rated '12'), it was in no way crude.

The depiction of 1982 Sheffield invited comparisons with other period dramas set in the recent past, such as *Call The Midwife,* but although *Brief Encounters* was wonderful exposure for the Ann Summers party plan business, it also emphasised how long it had been running, virtually unchanged.

It did change in 2021 though, when it was rebranded as The Sisterhood, and party hosts were renamed ambassadors. Discussing the revamp with *The Sun*, Jacqueline Gold reminisced about the project's early days: "I took my idea to the all-male, middle-aged board of directors," she said. "One of the bosses stood up, threw his pen on the table and said, 'Well this isn't going to work, is it? Women aren't even interested in sex!' – which said more about his sex life than it did my idea. But I managed to get the funding, then I advertised in the *London Evening Standard* to recruit women to throw the parties and I personally trained them."

The Ann Summers party was such a winning idea that it inevitably attracted competitors. I was once contacted by a chap who intended targeting straight men with a similar concept. The fact that I didn't hear from him again, nor can I now find any trace of his business online, suggests this wasn't a runaway success. I flippantly asked if he planned calling his prospective business 'Man Summers' but sadly he didn't (although a party plan firm aimed at gay men, called Jonny Winters, was launched in the UK in 2013).

Ann Summers started the new millennium the same way it ended the previous one: on top. Its name was synonymous with sex toys, raunchy lingerie, and hen night paraphernalia and it had become a generic term for a certain kind of shop which comedians could drop into their routine, fully confident their audience would get the joke: "I went into Ann Summers and asked the girl if the underwear was satin. She said 'No, you cheeky bugger, they're new'."

Not content with its market-leading position, Ann Summers was still growing in 2000. It acquired mainstream underwear retailer Knickerbox that year and also opened its first store in Ireland. But its expansion was being curtailed by Jobcentre Plus, the organisation charged with running job-seeking and social security services in the UK at that time. Jobcentre Plus had banned recruitment adverts for 'the Ann Summers category' so in 2003 the retailer instructed its legal team to fight the ruling in the courts.

Ann Summers estimated that if it was forced to use private recruitment agencies then a company of its size – which had 82 shops, 8,300 employees, and 7,500 party planners at that time – would end up with additional costs of over £250,000 a year. Mr Justice Newman found in favour of the firm, commenting that the policy was both "irrational and unlawful".

As well as helping Ann Summers, this ruling also proved beneficial to every other business operating in the sector.

Ann Summers was not afraid of using the legal system to protect itself in other ways: although the rabbit vibrator – made famous in US TV series *Sex And The City* – was well known in the industry, Ann Summers trademarked the name Rampant Rabbit for its versions of the design.

While it's usually seen as positive for rights owners if the public use brand names as generic descriptions – such as Biro or Hoover – Ann Summers, quite understandably, drew the line at rivals calling their own rabbits 'rampant' in their advertising, so it sent out Cease and Desist notices in 2004 to a number of firms it considered to be infringing its trademark.

A spokesperson for the firm said at the time that the Rampant Rabbit was its most successful product and "there will always be competitors offering imitations and trying to claw sales from Ann Summers… If a company is offering a rabbit toy they cannot claim that it is the Rampant Rabbit. Our campaign is to rid the web of references to Rampant Rabbit that are not truly justified and indeed breach trademark law."

While the firm declined to say how many competitors were targeted in the campaign, it did say – with no trace of irony – that abuse of its trademark was "rampant".

To the person on the street, Ann Summers has always been the racy face of retail, but its marketing seems to have been more playful in previous years.

For instance, as part of its National Orgasm Week campaign in 2004, it created an online ad which spoofed male motorists' unwillingness to ask for directions when they got lost. A spokesperson explained: "We discovered that less than 20% of people had had their best sex ever in the last 12 months and we wanted people to pledge to put the record straight. We had in-store pledge boxes and pledge leaflets in all of our stores and an online pledgeometer too – over the two weeks that we promoted the campaign over one million people pledged!"

A rather convoluted concept perhaps, but there's no arguing with the outcome.

Ann Summers was also at the forefront of new technology, being one of the first high street retailers to embrace the mobile space with the launch of wap.annsummers.com in June 2005. WAP – not to be confused with American rapper Cardi B's song of the same name – stood for Wireless Application Protocol, and it allowed mobiles to access the internet and the new Ann Summers mobile site, which included sex tips, product information, sexy stories, still and moving pictures, ringtones, and a 'money-off' in-store voucher.

Gordon Lee, marketing director at the time, commented at the launch: "We already use multiple routes to engage consumers. We're the largest party plan organiser in the UK, our website is one of the most successful on the internet, we are the number one pleasure retailer on the high street with in excess of one hundred prime locations, and our mail order business delivers more than 1,500 orders a week. The mobile space is the next place we want to be and it will be fully integrated into all elements of our existing operation. By putting Ann Summers content onto the mobile phone screen, we are extending the brand, and by selling the content we are adding an additional revenue stream."

Yes, 1,500 orders a week was considered a decent number back in 2005, and while we're on the subject of additional revenue streams, Ann Summers found another in 2007: branded vending machines. With the UK introducing a ban on indoor smoking, Luminar Leisure, owners of the Oceana and Liquid nightclubs, attempted to replace revenue lost from cigarette dispensers by installing machines containing saucy sweets, forfeit cards, lube, and even Rampant Rabbits, into six of its venues and it had plans to add more.

"The products are being purchased mainly by women but are also proving popular with party groups such as stag or hens," said a spokesperson for Luminar. "These new machines are not only adding to the fun club experience, but sales have also been very encouraging."

Ann Summers CEO Jacqueline Gold said the initiative guaranteed clubbers the perfect end to a night out: "From a woman's perspective, unlike anything else you might take home with you, this one is guaranteed to perform, will look as good the morning after, and won't lie about calling you," she quipped.

Ann Summers revamped its signature product in 2011, adding new varieties and giving them descriptive names. Like episodes of *Friends*, its Rampant Rabbits were now known as The Silicone One, The Thrusting One, The Rotating One, The Big One, The Little Shaking One, and The Twisted One. The firm simultaneously revised the products' packaging with a clever new logo: an upside down 'R' with ghosted echoes either side, resembling a stylised rabbit's head in motion.

"The previous packaging of our vibe range didn't give customers a very easy method of shopping," buying director Gary Donoghue told me. "The amount of newness we've got going into our toys this season has been dramatic and because of that we wanted to look at how we segmented our offer. We've come up with a brand-new packaging concept not only for Rampant Rabbit but also for our core sex toys. It's based on colour coding, which is going to make it easier for customers to go to the zone they want to find, and the boxes are now going to give respect to the merchandise.

"There is so much technology and innovation within these products that we've probably undersold them in the past. Quality is paramount to us and our packaging probably hasn't always done the best job it could have. We hope the new segmentation, combined with the new packaging, will make it much easier to understand what's behind the products and why the prices are different."

This new range of Rampant Rabbits featured in that year's Autumn/Winter catalogue, but they were just part of the story. "Every single category has changed in the new catalogue," added Donoghue. "We are looking to reclaim the edge in sexiness again and we've introduced two new categories, Sexcessories and Clubwear. With regard to Sexcessories – a name which we have trademarked – we've always done cuffs, the occasional whip, and underbed restraint but they've been dotted around the store with no real focus."

This initiative was to prove well timed, as we'll see…

Donoghue continued: "Sexcessories will be a destination zone in our stores and online and it will be categorised into three sub-brands: Decadence, which is softer; Diva for light bondage and more experimental elements; and finally Dominatrix, for the role-playing aspects and true bondage elements. This will be a one-stop destination centre in our stores. The new focus for Ann Summers is on reenergising our market leadership and being the sexiest brand on the high street."

Donoghue also explained that the firm was starting to be taken seriously by the mainstream media: "We were engaging fairly recently with the fashion press as we have started to change the balance of our lingerie range," he told me. "It is still cemented in the Ann Summers heritage but it is now taking on some of the fashion elements which our customers said they wanted.

"As a consequence of one of those meetings, the fashion editor of *Telegraph Online* wrote an amazing article headed 'Is that you, Ann Summers?' – it was the perfect article because she was taking another look at us and she was enthused by what she was seeing. We want people to re-engage with the brand so we used it as the tagline at the end of our Autumn Winter 11 lookbook and the response from journalists has been quite stunning. The important thing is the fashion element is only part of the whole though. We are not saying we are now a fashion lingerie business – we are Ann Summers."

It certainly was. That same year it came up with a cheeky ad campaign inspired by Marks & Spencer's famous sandwich, crisps, and drink Meal Deal. The Ann Summers version consisted of window posters and adverts emblazoned with 'Your S&M', 'Squeal Deal' and 'It's Not Just Sex, It's Ann Summers Sex'.

It was reported that M&S was taking legal advice, so Ann Summers prematurely cancelled the promotion. But the publicity surrounding the row probably resulted in more people being made aware of the campaign than if M&S had just looked the other way and allowed it to run its course.

Ann Summers discovered that a less controversial – and far cheaper – way of grabbing column inches was to farm its social media followers: just ask a question on Facebook and make some sense of the answers, preferably in the form of a listicle. If you've not encountered that term before, the Wikipedia explanation cannot really be bettered: 'A short-form of writing that uses a list as its thematic structure but is fleshed out with sufficient copy to be published as an article'.

A perfect example of this came in February 2014 when Ann Summers asked its 385,000 Facebook followers what their worst Valentine's Day present had been. The top ten answers included a Jeremy Clarkson autobiography, an ice scraper for the car, a loaf of bread, and washing up gloves.

This listicle would, in itself, have picked up some media traction but Ann Summers gave it added oomph by having CEO Jacqueline Gold appear at the chain's Bluewater branch where she very generously allowed women to trade-in unwanted Valentine presents for lingerie and sex toys.

How many unwanted gifts were traded in and what Ann Summers subsequently did with them was not recorded, but the initiative seemed to be for a good cause.

And speaking of causes, you are unlikely to have heard of LARGE CAUSE, unless you are or were an industry insider, but it presented a far bigger threat to the Ann Summers business model than an obscure website passing off its generic rabbit vibes as 'rampant'.

A little background is called for first though. If you or I decide to open an Ann Summers-style shop, all we have to do is find an empty store – not exactly difficult these days – and fill it with lingerie, lotions & potions, hen night novelties, and a selection of sex toys, right?

Wrong.

The UK requires stores that carry a 'significant degree' of 'sex related articles' to be licensed by their local authority. Should such a licence be granted, the council will impose a number of restrictions upon the successful applicant. These might include limiting the store's opening hours, blacking out the windows so passers-by cannot see inside, keeping records of everyone who enters the shop (by retaining CCTV footage for a certain period of time), and even stipulating what words can be used in the shop name.

It gets worse. Applying for a licence will require a fee – which can be thousands of pounds – to be paid, which is *not* refundable should the application prove unsuccessful. And if it is successful, that same fee has to be paid every year to the council.

Sounds a lot of hassle, right? Far easier to just sell slightly less 'sex related articles' than whatever a 'significant degree' is – except the interpretation of the phrase depends on your geographical location, and it encompasses more than just the number of items on sale.

A shop is required to be licensed if 'a significant degree' of its stock *or* display space is given over to, *or* its sales *or* profits are derived from, sex related articles. But there is no national 'standard' definition of what any of these terms mean, so it is left to individual councils to decide their own criteria.

As a result, a store in one town could be trading quite happily without a licence but an identical one ten miles away could face prosecution. And stores were prosecuted.

In June 2007, the owner of a York adult store was fined £14,000 and also ordered to pay the prosecution's costs for trading as a sex shop without a licence. Council officials claimed the store needed to be licensed due to the large quantity of erotic and sexual items on display.

The shop was raided in October 2006 and about 17% of the ground floor stock was considered erotic or sex-related while an upper level – which was protected by three warning signs – contained an estimated 60% of erotic content. The shop owner disputed these figures, saying the council had included non-erotic items such as hen night novelties and every single item of PVC clothing in its count, and that the correct percentage was around 38%, but this was still well in excess of the council's acceptable figure: 10%.

The shop owner appealed against the size of the fine, citing back issues of *ETO* which detailed much smaller fines other retailers had incurred for more serious offences. Judge Tom Cracknell, sitting with two magistrates, agreed and reduced the fine to £2,000.

Other authorities around the UK took different views, as we discovered in 2009 when *ETO* features editor Paul Smith conducted a comprehensive survey of councils' licensing officers. That figure of 10% was the lowest (ie the most draconian) in the UK, with a more typical amount being between 25% and 35% but most councils claimed they looked at each case on its own merits.

Which sounds fair, until you consider its implications in this context.

"This constitutes infinitely movable goalposts with no guarantee of consistency within a local authority's control zone, let alone against neighbouring councils," Paul concluded.

Annual fees also varied widely around the UK, with Castle Point Borough Council being the lowest (£500 per year) and Westminster City Council being the highest (£29,102 per year). Ann Summers branches were not licensed, so they did not have to black out their windows or fit a 'buzz to enter' front door, yet an independent store with a similar stock portfolio in the same street might have to comply with these and other requirements *and* pay almost £30k a year for the privilege.

Ridiculous, you might think, but that was the situation in Brewer Street in London's Soho in 2009. And eventually a group of the area's licensed retailers got together and formed a campaign group to do something about it.

LARGE CAUSE – an acronym for the rather awkward phrase Licensed Adult Retail Group Encourage Councils Abolish Unlicensed Sex Establishments – wanted authorities to adopt a uniform approach to licensing, and it claimed that under the Local Government (Miscellaneous Provisions) Act 1982, the Brewer Street branch of Ann Summers should be required to apply for a sex shop licence, so it brought a private prosecution against the store.

If the prosecution had been successful then, in addition to Ann Summers itself, it would have had far-reaching consequences for other unlicensed stores, online retailers, and maybe even party planners – some of whom would have been deriving more than 'a significant degree' of their sales or profits from sex related articles.

And it looked like the LARGE CAUSE case had been given a boost by a Jacqueline Gold profile piece on the *Telegraph.co.uk* website on 8th November 2009. Readers were informed that Ann Summers sold two million Rampant Rabbit vibrators, which retailed at around £50 each, per annum. If those figures – and others in the article stating that the chain's annual sales were £128m at that time – were accurate, then it implied that a staggering 78% of Ann Summers' overall sales came from sex toys, which certainly sounded like a 'significant' amount of sex related articles, though obviously not all sales were made through its retail stores.

The industry waited impatiently for the case to reach court. Marketing campaigns, expansion plans, and shop openings were put on hold. Overreacting? Not really, not when there was the possibility that the definition of what a sex shop actually is could have been agreed and a legal precedent set.

You can probably guess that that wasn't what happened.

A hearing took place at the City of Westminster Magistrates Court, London, on 11th February 2010, but those expecting District Judge Michael Snow to rule on whether the Ann Summers branch in Brewer Street should be classed as a sex shop – and, almost by definition, whether the entire Ann Summers chain should be too – would go home disappointed.

The judge rejected the private prosecution on three separate points, but they were related to who was bringing the prosecution and their reasons for doing so, rather than the nature of the case, and the evidence against Ann Summers was not even heard.

LARGE CAUSE released a statement after the case, saying: "Unfortunately, due to the complexities of law and pre-trial errors, our case failed and therefore no one is any closer to knowing what proportion of sex articles makes up a 'significant degree' before a shop is classed as a sex shop and therefore requires a license or is deemed to be trading illegally. According to the judge only a government office or council have the authority to bring a prosecution, and it is clear they don't seem to have the desire or funds to do so."

Jacqueline Gold was delighted by the outcome, saying: "This prosecution was ill conceived and never had any chance of succeeding. Ann Summers' successful trading model from 144 stores in the UK is accepted in 132 Local Authority Areas across the UK. Landlords in high streets and premier shopping centres compete to have Ann Summers open shops in their area. The judgment and the judge's words will ensure that anyone who might in future contemplate such a prosecution will be well advised to think carefully before embarking on such a course."

And that was the end of that, but some of the same stores that made up the campaign group were back in court in May 2012 seeking a judicial review against Westminster City Council's annual licence fees, alleging they were being used for purposes other than administration. The stores argued that EU laws which came into force in 2009 prevented local authorities from charging fees over and above the actual costs of administering the licensing process.

In this case, at least, the stores were more successful and, to cut a long story very short, annual licence fees did come down, not just in Westminster (where they plummeted from £29,102 to £2,500 per annum) but around the UK as a whole, as many councils pre-empted legal action from other licensed stores by voluntarily dropping their fees.

When it comes to popularising sex toys in the UK, Ann Summers has undoubtedly been a force for good. So too has Jacqueline Gold, who has done much to legitimise the sector as a whole, acting as a figurehead and frequently popping up in the financial press, making speeches at gatherings of business leaders, and championing other female-run enterprises through her social media channels.

Like most specialist retail chains, Ann Summers has experienced tough times in recent years, and it underwent a 'restructuring' in 2020. Its changing fortunes can be tracked by the store counts mentioned in this chapter's historic quotes, but while it might not have the number of stores it once did – who does? – it's still a familiar sight on the British high street and whether I arranged the chapters of this book alphabetically, chronologically, or in order of importance, Ann Summers was always going to be number one.

"For a woman, the experience must have been a bit like going into a shop which had the lights turned off with a load of heavy breathing men behind the counter…"

According to the Office for National Statistics (ONS), online transactions made up 27.1% of all retail sales in the UK in January 2022. The highest figure ONS ever recorded was 37.8%, which was in January the previous year when Britain was still grappling with restrictions aimed at curtailing the spread of COVID-19.

ONS does not, unfortunately, compile stats specifically on sex toys but I imagine the percentage of that sector's online sales is significantly higher than that of traditional retail sales, and has been for some time.

For many of us, purchasing an item as intimate as a sex toy will be a considered decision that involves all the senses. It should have visual appeal, the odour of the material should be neutral rather than noticeable, the device should be pleasing to the touch, and ideally it shouldn't be so loud that next door can follow your progress ("She shouldn't be long, she's put it on the high setting now…"). We'll leave out taste for now, though I'm sure someone in a lab is developing that too…

You'd therefore expect the obvious place to choose such a product, and compare it to its rivals, would be in a traditional retail setting, particularly if the location has a salesperson who is friendly, helpful, and knowledgeable about the products on display. And you'd be right. But it's a sex toy. And not everyone is comfortable revealing to complete strangers what tickles their fancy (many are, of course, and there are places on the internet for them to do just that – but this is not their story).

Buying online therefore has great appeal. The consumer can choose from far more products than even the biggest high street retailer can showcase, and have the object of their desire brought to their door in a plain brown box, usually the next day, for a price that will always be competitive. And under the UK's Distance Selling Regulations, the consumer can generally send the product back within 14 days if it fails to live up to expectations.

Offering products for sale outside of a conventional retail setting is nothing new, of course. Prior to the internet, the term used to describe such transactions was mail order, and it is generally believed that the first proponent of this was entrepreneur Pryce Pryce-Jones, who set up the Royal Welsh Warehouse in Newtown, Powys, in 1861 which used parcel post to deliver Welsh flannel to customers all over the world.

One hundred years later it was possible to buy condoms and other intimate products from the 'classified' pages of publications that would accept such advertising, and in return for sending these specialist suppliers a stamped self-addressed envelope. readers could receive a catalogue through the post, showcasing a whole new world of exotic devices.

General mail order catalogues were huge at this time, so consumers were familiar with the concept. Publications hundreds of pages thick from firms such as Littlewoods, Great Universal Stores, Freemans, Grattan, and Kays were a common sight in millions of households.

Although items in the catalogues frequently cost more than on the high street, they could be paid for in 20 interest-free instalments, collected weekly by a local agent, and the catalogues contained almost everything a growing family could need. From fun things for youngsters to furniture for oldsters, but those in search of 'marital aids', as sex toys were frequently referred to back then, by post would have to deal with those firms in the classified ads.

But as we approached the new millennium, a revolution was charging towards us.

Ann Summers' website says the firm began trading online in 1999, but I was able to find a capture of the site from December 1996 in which it described itself as 'The ultimate sex superstore'.

The text on the home page claimed it specialised in the design, manufacture, and sale of glamourous lingerie, personal products, and adult material. 'On this site is the largest selection on the Internet, which is updated on a regular basis,' it added. 'Further sites of a sexual nature are under construction, so keep slipping through the net and reveal a Sexual Experience you will never forget!'

Hmm.

After clicking 'Enter the Ann Summers experience', visitors were presented with four options: Sex Toys, PVC Rubber etc, Lingerie, and Main Order Form. Only the latter link on this slice of history still functioned at the time of writing. It contained enough space for 10 items to be ordered, and buyers could either print out the form and fax it (after completing their credit card details) or post it (if paying by cheque or money order) or they could click on the Order button. Consumers were required to pay a whopping £4 postage for the first item ordered and £1 for each additional one.

Below the main options were a selection of third-party links, most prominently a pair of strip ads. Literally. The top one promised: 'The all new strip show live on the internet. No downloading software! Appears immediately. Talk with her – tell her what you want' and the one below it followed the same theme: 'Internet live sex show. Lesbian show. No downloading of software. Straight to your screen!'

The site had a more sophisticated look by 2000, and as well as requesting a catalogue, booking a party, finding the location of their nearest store, and shopping online, visitors could find out more information about being an organiser and download screensavers and virtual postcards. The strip ads were gone. Ann Summers had upped its game, which was just as well as it was about to be joined by a fiercely ambitious competitor.

Lovehoney was formed in December 2001 by Richard Longhurst and Neal Slateford, who met at Future Publishing in Bath. Future was a hugely successful publisher of consumer magazines – I had a brief stint there myself in the 1990s – and Richard had been editor of *PC Format* and *.net*, the latter being the first magazine about the internet.

Neal joined Future in a business development role, focusing on the firm's websites, and prior to this he was a producer/remixer in the music industry. He worked with both Minogues and even had a hit himself, under the name DNA, with a remix of Suzanne Vega's *Tom's Diner*, which went to number one in 11 countries and sold some six million copies.

Richard went on to develop a shopping portal called 2020 Shops, which was a directory of more than 1,000 user-reviewed shopping sites, but he really wanted to run one of his own: "For a long time Neal and I had the idea of doing an online store," Richard told me in 2004 when I first interviewed the pair. "Initially it was going to be a kitsch toy store with things like punching nuns and Austin Powers dolls but with the success of *Sex and the City* it was pretty obvious that there was a huge demand for adult toys in general and women's toys, such as vibrators, in particular.

"We also reasoned that there would be a lot of people who would prefer to buy products of this nature online. There aren't sex shops in every town, and even if there was one in your town, you might be a little nervous about going in and buying something. Buying online is completely anonymous for the customer, and we could have a bigger product range with keener prices, so sex toys were ideal products to sell online."

The online competition at the time did not cause the pair too many sleepless nights, as Neal explained: "We looked at the sites that were out there and thought that many of them were pretty ropey and that we could do a better job of making something that would be more appealing to females."

Lovehoney's site was indeed noticeably different to its contemporary competitors. Its name was written in a 'fun' font and there was a cartoon of the site's host, 'Honey' – a swinging sixties-inspired redhead with a beehive – at the top of the home page.

"The thrust was to steer the site away from being semi-pornographic," added Richard. "Many of the existing websites at that time were aimed at men – 'buy this and stick it up your girlfriend/wife' – and they would have cheesy, scanned-in pictures of pouting lingerie models, with just a product listing, providing no information. Or it would be on a black background and you couldn't read the text, or there were badly written product descriptions…

"For a woman, the experience must have been a bit like going into a shop which had the lights turned off with a load of heavy breathing men behind the counter. So we got decent product pictures, described what the products do, provided advice on how to clean the toys, and which ones were too noisy to use in a flat, and highlighted the rabbits used by Charlotte and Samantha in *Sex and the City*. Because of our internet backgrounds, we had a pretty decent handle on how to make a website. We knew we could do it better than anyone else."

According to the pair, one of the reasons behind the early success of the business was the name, which went against the then-trend for online stores to call themselves after combinations of keyword-rich phrases, such as 'Erotic Sex Toy Dildo Dong Store', designed to attract the attention of search engines: "The inspiration for our name was a 1970s Russ Meyer film called *Mud Honey*," said Neal. "We played around with it and came up with Lovehoney and decided to create the Honey character. We wanted a name that sounded a bit sexy but which was also something you could use without embarrassment in conversation. 'Where did you get that?' 'Oh I bought it at Lovehoney.' You might not want to say you bought it at Sex Shop Something Or Other."

Richard and Neal weren't the only 'outsiders' moving into the industry in the early noughties. Apollo Sales, a B2B distributor, was formed in 2002 by chartered accountant Rod Thomas and software developer Simon Early. Thomas told me in 2004: "We were looking for a business to do together. We did a lot of homework, looking at different opportunities, and we decided that we wanted to be in the adult market. It fitted a lot of the criteria that we had established. It was a completely commercial decision. We felt it was a very strong, growing market that was on the verge of becoming mainstream, changing from being very male-focused, hard-edged, and not concerned about quality or packaging, to a marketplace that was far more focused on couples and women, where quality of product and presentation was much more important."

Their combined knowledge of the industry was minimal, but they didn't see that as a problem: "I've been in business for 25 years, and much of the systems, processes, organisation, and management is no different whatever the product is," Thomas said.

Apollo was one of the first distributors to offer its trade customers a shop-in-a-box: an ecommerce site that was pre-loaded with every product the supplier carried, complete with images, product descriptions, and prices. All the new trader had to do was buy a domain name and arrange hosting and online payment processing. If that was too much like hard work, Apollo would – for a fee – even do the fulfilment. It allowed literally anyone to become an online sex toys retailer.

Other firms, including Net 1on1 (the B2B arm of online retailer Sextoys.co.uk), were offering budding entrepreneurs even easier routes into the market via 'white label' sites that the customer promoted as their own. Net 1on1 started its programme in 2001 and by 2004 it had over 600 affiliates. A spokesperson for the company said at the time: "Affiliate programmes are generally perceived as a way of earning a few bob but no real money. This is simply not the case. It is entirely possible to earn over £2,000 from commission sales per month, as do some of our affiliates."

But while it had never been easier to get into the market, it had never been harder to get noticed. In addition to the flood of homegrown sites that had appeared, there were also numerous European operators targeting UK consumers. Suddenly the marketplace had become uncomfortably crowded. But there is always room – in every market – for a new entrant if it brings something different to the party.

And a South Wales couple certainly did that in early 2006. They opened an online sex toy store that was only looking to attract married customers. They got the idea after going away for their 10th wedding anniversary and visiting a sex shop for the first time. Shocked at the prices and the 'pornographic' nature of many of the products on sale ["Pornography? What, here, in a sex shop?"], the husband came up with the idea of opening a Christian site.

"At first I thought he was mad," his wife told BBC News online, "but then God changed my opinion and I thought it was a great idea." After seeking advice from church leaders and getting their support, they decided to go ahead with the store. "It's all based on sex within a marriage and we offer advice, discussion, and the shop," she added. "We want to strengthen marriages and sex is an important part of that."

She said that people were shocked when they first heard about a Christian sex toy site but, after considering the concept, they realised what a good idea it was. Although they were also told that they were working for Satan and would be going to Hell.

The site received a fair amount of coverage at launch, but Ann Summers found out that not all publicity is good publicity the following year, when *The Retail Bulletin* and specialist website testing company SiteMorse released details of testing it had conducted on the websites of 100 high street retailers. Automated testing took place on the first 125 pages of each site to generate a ranked table. The final table showed that only seven sites achieved what SiteMorse regarded as a good score of seven out of 10, and only 25% achieved a score of five out of 10.

Ann Summers was named as the worst retailer, and SiteMorse founder Lawrence Shaw commented on this, and the recently announced £2m investment into an Ann Summers bingo website: "Every page fails on accessibility (for visually impaired people) and every page fails on code quality. It should decide what's the most relevant thing to commit its investment to. And we don't think it is bingo."

As painful as that must have been to hear, its ambitious rival Lovehoney then took the fight to the sector Ann Summers dominated – party planning – by making a 'six-figure' investment in lingerie and sex toy party planners BlueBella.

"Lovehoney and BlueBella are perfectly placed to give modern women a fresh alternative to the tacky adult home parties they've had until now," said Lovehoney's Richard Longhurst.

BlueBella founder Emily Bendell added: "Companies such as Jamie at Home and Body Shop have shown that there is a huge demand for the right kind of products at the right kind of home party."

The deal gave BlueBella party planners exclusive access to Lovehoney products and Ann Summers' former party plan director Janet Mudge was brought in to drive sales and recruitment.

Lovehoney further broadened its reach in May 2011 when it acquired the domain name, trademark, and customer database of *BeCheeky.com*, an online lingerie and swimwear retailer which fell into liquidation two months previously.

"The purchase of *BeCheeky.com* will help us reach a more mainstream audience through media outlets currently denied to *Lovehoney.co.uk*," said Richard Longhurst pointedly. "Media nervousness and a general sniffiness towards adult retail has often proved a barrier for *Lovehoney.co.uk*."

Lovehoney celebrated its tenth anniversary in April 2012 and I visited the firm's Bath HQ for an in-depth interview with founders Neal Slateford and Richard Longhurst. A lot had changed since my last visit eight years previously. In 2004 Lovehoney consisted of four full-time and two part-time staff but by 2012 its head count was 75. It was fulfilling around 50,000 orders a month and its previous year's turnover was £13.5m.

The warehouse had more stock than I'd ever seen in one place before and the offices echoed with lively conversations as I was given the tour. I was surprised to see a bustling customer service area, where a group of headset-wearing staff were taking orders and chatting to customers.

I said I thought one of the benefits of being an online retailer was you didn't have to interact with the pesky public, but Longhurst soon shot that down: "Customer service is something we have hung our hats on ever since we started," he told me. "Back then the industry had a bad reputation for customer service. I remember looking at websites before we launched Lovehoney and they'd say things like, 'We will send your order when we get around to it and if it's not exactly the same as you see on the website, well that's essentially tough. No returns, no refunds, we don't want to hear from you'."

He continued: "We are the opposite. We want to hear from our customers. We want to know what they enjoy, what they like about our service and what they dislike so we can improve it. We are all about the idea of sexual happiness and part of that is making the customer happy with their purchases and the service they receive from Lovehoney. The team that is down there have just one instruction: make the customer happy. We don't have scripts or lots of rules and we don't really teach them anything other than do whatever it takes to make the customer happy.

"When we recruit new staff we have to spend quite a long time deprogramming them from things they have learned in their last customer service job. For example, they will start from a position of being suspicious of customers, that they are trying to rip us off: 'I don't have permission to give a refund or a replacement order' or 'You have to wait two weeks for your order to turn up before I can re-send it'.

"All that rubbish is out of the window. Do whatever it takes to make the customer happy. If they ring up the day after their parcel should have been delivered and they want to have it re-sent, just do it. Do what will make them happy and they will come back and tell their friends and we end up with this virtuous circle of customers and growth."

Our conversation turned to the BlueBella investment and Neal candidly explained that Lovehoney had first entered the party plan sector in 2004 but had been "crap" at doing it. He said: "We thought we could use the Lovehoney principal and make our party plan better than anyone else's. We had better products and better prices so the reps will make more money: how hard can it be? The answer was really, really hard. We didn't really understand that the party plan business was all about motivating the reps and managing them rather than the products. We decided we were not very good at it, so we stopped, but we still wanted to be in that space."

Richard added: "BlueBella had already built up a pretty decent head of steam. They had more than 100 reps and were looking for an investment and a partner that could help them with fulfilment, computer systems, product development, and branding, which are all things we could do. There were lots of reasons for doing it: to reach people in a way that Lovehoney wasn't reaching them; to get Lovehoney products in front of those people; and to cause another problem for Ann Summers in a part of the business that it had totally to itself."

Richard also elaborated on the reasons behind the acquisition of *BeCheeky.com*: "That was an opportunity that came up but we had been thinking of launching a lingerie website. Partly because we have a warehouse full of lingerie, and we could do with another avenue to sell it, but also because a lot of places wouldn't let Lovehoney advertise due to the nature of some of the products. You can't go on the shopping search engines for example, and you can't take adverts in some magazines. And when a lingerie customer comes on to the Lovehoney site they might be put off by some of the sex toys…

"Also, some lingerie suppliers wouldn't sell to Lovehoney, because they didn't want their nice knickers sold alongside our butt plugs. So there were lots of good reasons for launching a separate lingerie website. We were toying with calling it Lovehoney Lingerie at first, then we were developing a site called BeLucky, but then BeCheeky had its problems and went bust, giving us the opportunity to acquire a ready-made brand name and domain name."

But while Lovehoney was looking outwards, and taking the fight to other areas, it was facing more competition in its own backyard, especially from a relatively new rival called Bondara, whose founder and CEO, former investment banker Chris Simms, entered the market in 2007 via a rather unusual route: an eBay listing.

After he left the City, Chris decided to sell one of his surplus business suits on the online auction site. To his dismay, the tailor-made unworn suit only made 99p while the item listed next to it, a cheap ball gag, sold for £20. From such trifling incidents destinies are changed. Chris bought a few ball gags of his own and listed them. When eBay objected, and kept ending his auctions, Chris decided to create his own website.

I visited Bondara's impressively large HQ in August 2012, and it was clear that business was booming. It had a warehouse full of busy pickers and packers and a Royal Mail lorry was in the process of being filled with customer orders. This wasn't too surprising as my visit coincided with the absolute peak of the Fifty Shades Fever that was sweeping the UK – but more on that later.

Simms estimated his company was number three in the UK market at that time: "Ann Summers is number one and Lovehoney is number two," he said. "And there are clear gaps between all of us."

To go from a standing start to number three in the market in five years was quite an achievement but Simms was not one to blow his own trumpet – I had to practically beat the answer to my 'Where do you think you are in the market?' question out of him – and when discussing his progress he made it sound like anyone could have done it: "In 2007 Ann Summers was the big brand, the undisputed king of the industry, and I could see the potential that the up and coming Lovehoney had, but I felt there was a big gap between the top two and everyone else and that there was room for a number three to also do well."

Instead of dipping a toe in the water though, he went big: "Everything I'd earned in the City I put into the business," he said. "It all went on the building of the website and on stock. I was quite selective about what I bought though. Even now, a lot of our competitors offer a lot more products than us across the board. But I decided that if you choose well there is no point in overwhelming the customer with too many options. When it came to the design of the site, I looked at what colours weren't present – Ann Summers was quite dark and Lovehoney back then was browny-orange – and as there was nothing bright and pink I went for that."

Simms only had good things to say about the market leader: "I admire Ann Summers and it upsets me when I see competitors slagging them off," he said. "They forget that if Ann Summers didn't exist then nor would they. Ann Summers has made this industry acceptable, and it has allowed others to join in. I look up to Ann Summers."

The online space became even more crowded in October 2012 when sexual health charity the Family Planning Association (FPA) opened an online store. The FPA was formed in 1930 with the original remit of offering birth control advice to married couples, and it believed consumers would prefer to buy products from its site rather than 'unfamiliar' retailers, especially as any profits would go towards supporting its work.

As well as the 'serious' pharmaceutical names one might expect to see on the site, such as Durex and KY, over 100 industry brands were represented, with products ranging from a gold-plated butt plug to a Jac-Off masturbation pad.

"FPA has always recognised sexual pleasure as an essential element of good sexual health," said FPA's business development manager, Terry Hawkins. "As a well-known and trusted brand we think that people who aren't comfortable buying intimate products from unfamiliar retailers will want to shop with us. We hope they'll also like the added incentive of knowing that when they buy online, they're supporting our charitable work with young people, parents, vulnerable adults, and men and women across the UK."

The charity closed in 2019 but FPA still exists as a commercial entity, though its online shop now offers teaching aids and publications rather than sexual pleasure products.

One of the biggest sellers of sex toys today is Amazon – which we'll come to later – and the consumer can also source sex toys from eBay too. While this might not have seemed a particularly appealing proposition in the early days, when the auction site was mainly known for secondhand – the term 'pre-loved' is a bit icky in this context – goods, eBay is now just another selling platform.

While I browsed the 'sex toy' category after writing that last sentence, I found no private sellers among the 33,000+ listings, only businesses – including some well-known names – but I only scrolled through the first couple of pages, so they might be there.

The mechanics of online retailing have remained essentially the same since Pryce Pryce-Jones set up the Royal Welsh Warehouse in 1861 but in 2015 a new concept made its way to our shores from France: subscription boxes. Daring Box subscribers would be sent a parcel of pleasure products every two months but wouldn't know what it contained until they opened it. An annual subscription cost £195 for six boxes, and discovering the contents was seen as part of the fun for recipients.

While I could understand the appeal of the 'I wonder what we'll get' anticipation and appreciate the lack of effort required to enjoy it, I wasn't sure if a package of surprise sex toys was as sound a business model as, say, introducing people to different wines from around the world, but Daring Box was soon joined by Roomantics, JustUs Box, and Casanova's Box, and no doubt there were others I either didn't hear about or can't recall. And, never ones to spot a gap it didn't want to fill, Lovehoney introduced its own scheme in 2019 called Play Box.

Lovehoney is the perfect standard bearer for this chapter. It arrived not long after the new century and within 20 years it had become a huge concern, picking up innumerable trade and business awards along the way. During a May 2017 interview, Richard Longhurst told me: "Over the years the mainstream awards have helped get the Lovehoney name and the sex toy industry regarded on an equal footing with mainstream ecommerce businesses."

Neal Slater added: "It's very satisfying when you're nominated in something like the Retail Week Awards and the others in the category are people like John Lewis."

Almost as satisfying, they told me, as meeting the Queen and other senior royals at a reception at Buckingham Palace for winners of the Queen's Award for Enterprise in International Trade in 2016, after which their local Member of Parliament, Ben Howlett, visited the firm. Richard said: "He had a lot of intelligent questions and we had a fun time trying to find a product he would be photographed with. He didn't want the Rookie Prostate Massager and he wouldn't hold the Topco Perfect Ass either. But that's a good sign of how far Lovehoney has come, and the adult industry has come with it – that our MP spent an hour-and-a-half looking around the business and actually engaging with sex toys and posting on his own blog and Twitter that he'd done that."

While online retailers like Lovehoney have been taking bigger and bigger slices of the sales pie this century, they were practically given the keys to the bakery in March 2020 when the UK went into compulsory lockdown in an attempt to stop the spread of COVID-19.

With all 'non-essential' businesses forced to close, parcel delivery drivers had the roads to themselves as they ferried groceries, takeaways, and consumer goods – including sex toys – to the housebound. On 13th March of that year, a *MailOnline* article was headlined, rather inelegantly, 'Global sales of SEX TOYS have drastically boosted in sales due to the coronavirus pandemic'. The headline proved to be accurate – in content if not grammar – as, according to industry insiders, sex toys really were being shipped in record numbers during this time.

There are downsides to purchasing any product online, of course, such as ensuring someone is available to receive it and the hassle of returning it if it is less than satisfactory, but the well-heeled can avoid all this by employing a sex toy consultant, which is a bit like having a party planner devoted just to you. Your consultant will discuss your requirements in advance and then visit your home with a selection of samples for you to assess. You're under no pressure to buy as the consultant charges a fee for their time. Instead of you going to the shop, the shop comes to you. Now that's progress.

"Essentially all journalists are lazy. So if you can deliver to them a brilliant story with a great headline and a fantastic photo they will put it in their newspaper, magazine, or on their website."

In a 2014 article for *Forbes.com* about the difference between advertising and PR (public relations), Robert Wynne began with: "Advertising is what you pay for, publicity is what you pray for."

It's a snappy soundbite, and although it came from someone who describes himself as a 'public relations professional' that doesn't mean it isn't true. In a less concise nutshell, the difference between advertising and PR is: if I want to take out a full page in *The Guardian* newspaper to tell its readership how great I am it will cost me £18,000 (2021 ratecard), but if that same publication devotes a full page of editorial to me it will cost me nothing. As long as the story is positive of course – if the writer portrays me as a bit of a dick, it could cost me plenty.

Assuming I'm not a dick, the editorial page will not only save me the cost of a brand-new Volkswagen Polo (£18,575 at the time of writing), but it could also be significantly more effective than the advertisement. Returning to Robert Wynne's article, he quotes Michael Levine, author of the book *Guerrilla PR*, as saying: "The idea is the believability of an article versus an advertisement. Depending on how you measure and monitor an article, it is between 10 times and 100 times more valuable than an advertisement."

In other words, while it's easy to tell people positive stories about yourself, those stories will be more credible if someone else is telling them. But comparing the two forms of promotion was pretty tricky for sellers of sex toys – as Lovehoney's Richard Longhurst alluded to in the previous chapter – because so many branches of the media refused to help them spend their marketing budget. But PR can, on its own, be wonderfully effective. For instance, do you know the size of Tesla's advertising budget? It's actually zero, but is there anyone who doesn't know what a Tesla is?

A question I was often plaintively asked by other retailers was: "Why does Lovehoney get so much press coverage?"

Sometimes this question was asked by people with very similar business models to Lovehoney, who were selling similar products at similar prices, but the media was failing to beat a path to their door or asking them for products to include in their 'Top Ten Sexy Toys To Spice Up Valentine's Day' features.

The reason Lovehoney got so much coverage was that it knew what the media was looking for, and it provided it. Richard Longhurst told me in a May 2017 interview: "Essentially all journalists are lazy. So if you can deliver to them a brilliant story with a great headline and a fantastic photo they will put it in their newspaper, magazine, or on their website. And so we spent a lot of effort coming up with what we call 'wheezes' – inventive things that will give newspapers and magazines an excuse to write about us."

I bristled at Richard's use of the word 'lazy', suggesting the term 'overworked and underpaid' would be more appropriate, and Richard replied: "Efficiency is the economy of effort, Dale… I was as lazy as the next one."

So well written and targeted were Lovehoney press releases that the time-poor journalist could indeed just copy and paste their contents directly into layout software to create an instant story.

I first encountered a Lovehoney 'wheeze' in 2004, when it was just one of many websites selling sex toys. In June of that year, it sponsored a pink Reliant Robin, styled like Lady Penelope's FAB 1 Rolls Royce from *Thunderbirds*, which was raising money for the Breakthrough Breast Cancer charity. The two female co-drivers were embarking on a 4,000-mile journey to deliver free condoms and sex toys to Eastern Europe.

The article arrived fully formed, requiring very little editing to adopt into a house style, and it came with an image of one of the ladies, dressed in a vibrant pink jump suit, splayed across the bonnet of the car. Now what editor could resist that?

It was a foretaste of what was to come, with some of Lovehoney's greatest hits being its Rabbit Amnesty [sex toy recycling scheme], Britain's Sexiest Towns [the areas of the UK that buy the most sex toys] and its Design A Sex Toy competitions [this man has earned £x from his bright idea] chalking up acres of column inches.

As well as creating its own wheezes, anything topical was fair game. In 2005 it cashed in on the UK general election by running a viral marketing campaign inviting visitors to 'Forget about the policies and talk about the penises'.

The campaign asked visitors of a separate standalone site to vote for the party leader they would most like to have sex with. Or, if they didn't fancy any of the all-male three, to cast a vote for Jeremy Paxman instead. Voting results were presented in the form of amusingly animated penises, and voters were sent a Lovehoney discount voucher and entered into a competition to win an 'erection night' pleasure pack.

The site proved popular with the media: "It was a very cost-effective way for us to increase awareness of Lovehoney and add a significant number of subscribers to our mailing list," said Longhurst.

Lovehoney was one of the first adult retailers to successfully court the women's press and it was routinely mentioned whenever magazines such as *Cosmopolitan*, *Company*, or *Marie Claire* featured adult products, while its Britain's Sexiest Towns initiative allowed just about every local newspaper in the UK to run a sexy story with a local angle.

"We have deliberately created projects around PR ideas, imagining the headline and working back from that," Richard told me in 2012. "With Britain's Sexiest Towns we realised we were sitting on a wealth of data, years' worth of what people had bought and from which postcodes. With a bit of nerdery we could mash that up and create a Google map of where people are buying sex toys and who's sexy and who's not. The data was linked online so people would link back to Lovehoney and improve our search engine rankings."

Neal Slateford added: "Rabbit Amnesty was another one. People don't believe it's real but we genuinely do everything the project says we do: recycle the rabbits and donate to the World Land Trust. People ask us how we do our sex toy recycling. We just do it. Find a recycling centre, ask them if they will take vibrators and how much you have to pay and just do it. It's not rocket science."

This project was introduced in September 2007 and was trumpeted as the world's first sex toy recycling scheme. It gave consumers the opportunity to dispose of their old toys in a clean, green, responsible way while also purchasing a rabbit vibrator from the Lovehoney range at half price. For each rabbit returned through the scheme, Lovehoney pledged to donate £1 to the World Land Trust in support of the charity's tropical forest land purchase and protection projects.

If the goal behind the Rabbit Amnesty recycling scheme was to be widely applauded in the mainstream media then it certainly achieved its objectives, but flying under the radar of the 'eco' headlines was a bloody great stealth bomber: "Rabbit Amnesty was originally started to make Lovehoney more synonymous with rabbits," revealed Richard. "Thinking through the logic of who owns a rabbit in the UK and where they bought it from, many will have been bought from Ann Summers. So it was a way of saying to people that if you've got an old rabbit in your drawer, chances are you would have been an Ann Summers customer – but send it to us and we'll give you a new one for half price. As well as being brilliant PR, which was covered in

The Guardian, *Hippy Shopper* and all the green blogs, it was also a useful way of getting Lovehoney in front of Ann Summers' customers."

Lovehoney launched its Design A Sex Toy competition in 2006, which resulted in the creation of one of its signature products, the Sqweel. "Trevor [Murphy], the guy who designed Sqweel, now lives off the royalties from it in Toronto," Richard told me. "He used to live in a caravan in a field in Ireland. It's a fantastic story and it gave Lovehoney a point of difference in the UK. We had something no one else had. This gave us another massive PR hit and it led to the setting up of Lovehoney in the US, and it started our B2B business as we sell it into the trade in the US, Europe, Australia, and Asia."

All this coverage in the mainstream media did not go unnoticed by Lovehoney's competitors: some employed PR agencies and others appointed their own staff, and they too achieved some notable successes, particularly in getting their products placed in mainstream television programmes, but nobody appealed to print journalists like Lovehoney.

I would still hesitate to agree with Richard's earlier assertion that journalists are lazy, as they really are under immense pressure to bang out stories at a rapid rate, especially in the online space. So if a newsworthy Lovehoney story, complete with a suggested headline and eye-catching artwork, can be assembled quickly and with very little effort, a journalist with space to fill and a deadline to meet would need a good reason *not* to use it.

Sometimes relatively trivial stories went viral. For a brief period in April 2006, Nice 'n' Naughty became one of the most talked-about retail chains in the world.

The tale began with a simple local request for sponsorship: in this case it was Southport Cricket Trinity Cricket Club, which asked Nice 'n' Naughty (NNN) if it would sponsor its shirts for the coming season.

At the higher echelons of sport, sponsorship is a marriage of convenience where both parties benefit from the union. The sponsor gets its name associated with events or teams its target demographic cares about while the sport gets to balance its books and reward its participants – no matter how incongruous the marriage may be, such as when McDonald's or Budweiser sponsors a football tournament. At a local level however, sport sponsorship is more about putting something back into the community where the business is based. If a few extra customers get to hear about the business as well, that's a bonus. Usually.

As NNN had already taken a paid-for advertisement in the (deep breath) *Littlewoods Gaming Liverpool & District Cricket Competition League Handbook*, and NNN director Simon Prescott was a cricket supporter, the sponsorship deal was agreed. For a payment of around £1,000 NNN would have its name and logo on the club's shirts for the coming season.

If that had been it, the story may have picked up a few column inches in the sports section of the local paper. But a representative of the Littlewoods Gaming Liverpool & District Cricket Competition, sent out a blanket email to all club secretaries in the league in which every word was capitalised and bold, emphasising that this was a message to be taken seriously.

The email read, in full: "Following full consideration by the management committee of the Littlewoods Gaming Liverpool & District Cricket Competition, it has been decided that Southport Trinity Cricket Club must withdraw from their current sponsorship arrangements which are judged to be not in the interests of cricket and to be setting unacceptable standards particularly in relation to junior cricket. The club is considered to have made serious misjudgements with regard to this sponsorship. The management committee of the Littlewoods Gaming Liverpool & District Cricket Competition make clear that Southport Trinity Cricket Club will forfeit all points in any match if clothing bearing the logo of their current sponsor is worn at any time by any team."

This was despite the fact that the league had previously approved the deal, as well as taking NNN's paid-for advert in its handbook. Faced with losing its league status, just a week before the start of the season, Southport Trinity advised NNN that it would have to cancel the deal and repay the £1,000.

The story appeared in the *Liverpool Echo* and on the BBC's website and then went viral. I reckon part of the story's appeal was the opportunity it gave headline writers to show off their punning skills: it's just not cricket; club being run out of competition; league officials bowled over; league chairman stumped why club with junior sides would team up with sex shop; Southport Trinity to bail out of deal; adult shop hit for six etc. No, I didn't see them all, but I just know they existed.

Simon Prescott and Trish Murray of NNN appeared on Victoria Derbyshire's Radio 5 Live mid-morning programme on 13th April, when the story was discussed on air. At the end of it, even Victoria sympathised with the retailer. Her initial Maud Flanders-style 'Won't somebody think of the children?' reaction was negated by the discovery that the league itself was sponsored by a gambling operator, and other teams in the league had breweries as sponsors, and she was completely disarmed by the attitude of Simon and Trish. Instead of coming out fighting, complaining about injustice, double standards, hypocrisy etc, my main recollection of the interview was them saying how disappointed they were that the deal had been cancelled and that they hoped that one day they would be allowed to sponsor the club, like any other respectable business.

A representative of the English Cricket Board, which had ultimately been behind the decision, came across as a bit out of touch, however. Further radio interviews followed, plus a slot on that day's BBC TV News at six o'clock, and Simon put together a press release with his comments on the matter, emphasising that NNN had eight shops, employed 30 staff, had gained Investor in People certification, also sponsored other local sports teams in areas where it had shops, and that it had been voted 'ETO Adult Retailer of the Year' the previous year.

The story went on to appear on the websites of the BBC, BBC Sport, *The Telegraph*, *The Sun*, *The Mirror*, and being cricket-related, it was also picked up by websites in countries which play the sport, including *CNN* of India, Pakistan's *Daily Times*, South Africa's *Mercury*, and New Zealand's *Newswire*. As a footnote, Simon Prescott informed the club that despite the sponsorship deal being cancelled, it could still keep the £1,000.

A minor incident the following year saw Nice 'n' Naughty once again in the news. A quantity of sex toys had been stolen from its delivery vehicle, which had been parked on a street in Liverpool, prior to unloading its cargo for the opening of a new store. Thieves broke the window of the van to gain entry and made off with 36 rabbit vibes, 18 tubs of chocolate body paint, and 12 blow-up dolls.

With the theft happening close to Valentine's Day, the story made the front page of every local newspaper across the northwest, every local radio station picked up on it, and Simon Prescott took part in 10 live phone ins. It went on to appear in tabloids such as *The Sun*, *The Sport*, and *The Daily Star* and Prescott was quoted in one online report as saying: "The race is now on to import dozens of rabbits and blow-up dolls from our suppliers in Amsterdam. The business is extremely busy at the moment and it is crucial we get this stock replaced as quickly as possible, particularly as Valentine's Day is fast approaching. We are committed to our customers and I will ensure these shelves are filled as soon as possible. We will make sure we do not let anyone down."

Online retailer Sextoys.co.uk looked to be onto a winner in July 2007 when it sponsored Jodie Marsh's tour bus. The model and reality TV star was going to be spending the summer searching for a husband, and she had an MTV film crew recording her exploits for a series called *Totally Jodie Marsh: Who Will Take Her Up The Aisle?*, which promised to culminate with her marrying the chosen winner.

"Jodie loves our website," said a Sextoys.co.uk representative, "so we were the obvious choice to sponsor her bus for the tour. This was a great chance to showcase our brand across the country and to create awareness in a fun and enjoyable way."

Amazingly, the series did end with Marsh marrying. The lucky winner was Matt Peacock, an ex-boyfriend of fellow glamour model Jordan, though the couple separated before the year was out.

One of the smartest PR initiatives I witnessed came from French online retailer *Absoloo.com* in June 2012. Capitalising on the launch of the eagerly awaited PC strategy game *Diablo III*, Absoloo asked 'game widows' to visit its Facebook page and post a photograph of them holding a copy of the game. In return, they would receive a voucher for a free sex toy.

Lovehoney proved that *everything* was PR-able in April 2014, after it emerged that some members of Pendle Borough Council in Lancashire considered their new logo inappropriate. The logo – an inoffensive green heart – had been commissioned to celebrate the 40th anniversary of the authority, but some thought it to be too similar to Lovehoney's red heart logo.

One councillor said: "It really does concern me because do we want Pendle to share a logo with a sex shop like Lovehoney? I don't think we should be associated with that kind of thing", while another said the thought of seeing the logo all over the town had them "reaching for blood pressure medication".

Lovehoney was quick to exploit the rumpus by offering all councillors who objected to the design a free sex toy. "This just shows how far we have reached into the fabric of society, at least in Pendle," Richard Longhurst said in a press release.

Even coining a memorable phrase can result in extensive coverage. In 2015 Lovehoney revealed that it had received its biggest ever media response from a product that was neither unique to it nor even new to the market. The product was the Svakom Gaga, a vibrator that featured a light and a camera so users could shoot their internals.

At this point, a quote from *Jurassic Park* might come to mind ("Your scientists were so preoccupied with whether they could, they didn't stop to think if they should") but the Lovehoney PR machine triumphed by creating a new term to describe the product: the sex selfie stick. "Ever wondered what happens inside the body during climax?" asked the press release. "Now you can find out. It allows users to get to know their body in its entirety thanks to the remarkably clear footage this camera captures. Thanks to its FaceTime compatibility, sharing the view with your lover couldn't be easier – whether you're sat right next to each other or miles apart."

The idea came from Lovehoney's sex toy category manager Alice Little, who said: "The response was incredible. The world's media wanted to know more about the Gaga and the easiest way to do this was by linking to our video. Hundreds of sites used the story and embedded our video. It shows just what an appetite there is for sex product news if it is packaged in the right way."

The story appeared on sites such as *The Independent, Metro, Daily Mirror, Daily Mail, New York Daily News, Cosmopolitan, Marie Claire* and MTV, and the Lovehoney video of Annabelle Knight demonstrating how the toy works is still available on YouTube, where it has been seen over 5.6m times.

Where Lovehoney pioneered the 'We can turn anything into a news story about us' path to success, others inevitably tried to follow. Hot Octopuss (yes, that is how the firm spells its name) rose to prominence in industry circles in 2013 with the launch of Pulse, a male masturbation device.

Referring to Pulse as a 'guybrator' was always going to attract media attention but the firm also came up with a cunning stunt to capitalise on the England men's football team's disappointing 2-1 defeat to Italy in the 2014 World Cup. Under the pretext of 'an attempt to raise morale among the squad', Hot Octopuss couriered a box of its toys out to the boys. Adam Lewis, Hot Octopuss co-founder, said: "Every red-blooded man knows what a struggle it must have been for the boys without their WAGs, so we thought we'd send each of the players their own Pulse to the training camp in Brazil."

Whether the players received the devices, much less used them, I cannot say. But if they did, adding guybrating sessions to their ball-juggling routines failed to pay off on the pitch as the results of England's next two games were another disappointing 2-1 defeat, against Uruguay, followed by a tedious 0-0 draw against Costa Rica.

Still, at least the stunt allowed immature elements of the media to include the word 'wankers' in their headlines. Actually that might have been just me.

Upmarket Swedish sex toy brand Lelo picked up a decent amount of media coverage – though not all of it was necessarily favourable – for its rather unusual Pino launch campaign in December 2014. Pino was a vibrating cock ring, though Lelo – being an upmarket operation, as I said – called it a vibrating couples' ring and supplied it in a gift box along with a money clip and cufflinks, as it believed it would be an 'obvious' gift for bankers, executives, and businessmen.

"Pino is the ultimate stimulus package, the most exclusive couples' ring in the world and is aimed at the wolves of Wall Street and Gordon Gekkos of our communities," said Steve Thomson, Lelo's head of marketing. "They're rarely satisfied and always looking for new limits to push, so Pino is about meeting those demands and adding a new adventurism to their sex lives. Can you think of a more demanding group to design a sex toy for? For most of us, sex is one of the most wonderful, pleasurable experiences in our lives. In the male-dominated, testosterone-drenched context of banking, it's an obsession, and that perhaps explains the demands Lelo receives for delivery to financial institutions. Bankers are both proud of their sex lives but also want to make sure they're doing it right. Pino is kind of an external consultant in that respect."

The following year, the same company launched a product with a unique extra: free break-up 'insurance'. The Tiani 24k was a swanky version of Lelo's existing Tiani couples' toy, designed to be worn during intercourse. The vibe featured a ring of 24 karat gold and, as the ring is such an iconic symbol of commitment, Lelo explained, any couple who broke up within 12 months of purchasing a Tiana 24k could opt to replace it with a different product, such as a solo vibe.

The company said it was able to make this offer due to the positive impact its products had on relationships, though Steve Thomson wasn't expecting many claims: "Lelo is not simply about bringing people together, we're about keeping them together, and we're prepared to prove it," he said. "Lelo is a brand that's committed to enhancing the connection between partners and we have no hesitation in putting our money where our mouth is. We are confident our latest innovation can have a truly positive impact on the relationship of the owners."

In early 2016, the US office of Hot Octopuss was making headlines for – I shit you not – installing a 'GuyFi' male stress relief booth in Manhattan. The press release stated that 80% of Americans said they suffered from workplace stress and cited a *Time Out* report that claimed 39% masturbate in the workplace to alleviate this stress.

The GuyFi booth offered a high-speed internet connection and a privacy curtain, so office workers could de-stress in a 'more suitable' environment, away from their colleagues. "There's no denying that working a nine to five job can be stressful on both your mind and body, especially in a non-stop city like Manhattan," said Adam Lewis. "It's really important for guys to look after themselves so that they can stay healthy and focus properly on the task in hand. We're told time and time again how beneficial it is to have a break away from your desk. At Hot Octopuss we are all about looking for new solutions to improve everyday life and we feel we've done just that with the new GuyFi booth. We hope the city's men enjoy using the space we've created in whatever way they want. It's completely free of charge – all that we ask is they thank us when they get their promotion."

If the purpose of the story was to pick up coverage, then it worked. It attracted the attention of a stack of media outlets from *Mashabale* to *Metro*. The former's dismissive report said: "The company simply put a cloth over a phone booth in what amounted to a marketing gimmick. Inside was a chair and a laptop…" while *Metro* was more enthusiastic, ending with a poll which asked if its readers would use it. 34% chose 'I sure would, where is it again?' while 66% clicked the 'No, this is as depraved as it gets and I want more than a curtain before I do depraved things' option.

There was a tone of irritation in *Cosmopolitan*'s coverage however, which concluded: "What's not reported: how the fuck they clean this bad boy; who the fuck is responsible for cleaning it; how many idiots took this as a cue to start masturbating in other phone booths; and how much less stressful life was for all these super-stressed gentlemen after their little field trips. Call me when female masturbation booths exist and all the people who loved this idea hate that one."

And talking of *Metro*, which I was in the paragraph-before-last, I must mention the headline the publication chose for its April 2016 report on Lovehoney receiving Royal recognition, via the prestigious Queen's Award for Enterprise in International Trade, for its achievements.

Metro's online coverage was headlined: 'The Queen's endorsed the company behind the Rampant Rabbit' – which no doubt delighted the Lovehoney founders but I doubt Jacqueline Gold would have seen the funny side.

The headline was amended – I'd guess pretty hastily, judging by the result – to 'The Queen's endorsed the company behind a lot of sex toys'. It's a shame I used the phrase 'I shit you not' earlier as this would be an even more apt place for it.

The Lovehoney co-founders went on to meet the Queen, Prince Philip, and other senior royals at a reception at Buckingham Palace for Queen's Award winners in July 2016 and Neal Slateford commented: "It's a huge privilege for Lovehoney to be honoured by the Queen. The Queen is Britain's greatest trade ambassador and consumers trust a brand with her patronage. It just shows how far we have come as a company and how sex toys are becoming more and more mainstream."

But you don't have to be an international business with a multi-million-pound turnover that receives awards from the Queen to get media coverage, as Aylesford retailer Vibez Adult Boutique proved in September 2017. The store became one of the first in the UK to stock the sexbot created by Dr Sergi Santos and Arran Squire of Synthea Amatus.

'Samantha' was said to be the most advanced artificially intelligent sex robot ever to be sold in a shop. Retailing at £2,500, she featured eight different modes and 11 sensors that 'respond to touch'. Vibez owner Tracey Whitmore told *The Daily Star*: "Samantha is getting on really well with my customers, but she is causing a bit of a stir, I have to say. Customers have been talking to her, touching her, and squeezing her boobs regularly. The guys are going crazy for her. One guy yesterday actually made her orgasm just by stroking her."

Even a perceived injustice can result in a previously little-known company's name zooming around the world. The 2019 International Consumer Electronics Show (CES) was staged in Las Vegas from 8th – 11th January. An annual event, CES is where the world's largest technology brands, such as Sony, Microsoft, and Panasonic, unveil their latest innovations to the world's media, and in recent years one or two of the more switched-on sex toy brands – led by longtime exhibitor OhMiBod – have taken space.

One of the key features of CES is its awards, which are presented by the organisers, and in 2019 Lora DiCarlo's Osé personal massager was initially included in the CES 2019 Innovation Awards in the robotics and drone category. This award was subsequently rescinded as the organisers said they had made a mistake, and the nature of Osé meant it should never have made it through judging.

Do you think Lora DiCarlo's eponymous CEO accepted this disappointing news quietly? She absolutely did not, and the story was picked up by major news networks around the world. People who had never even heard of CES before suddenly became aware of Lora DiCarlo and what it made. 'We fought back,' the company said in an online post. 'The truth runs deeper than a simple processing error, and we recognised it for the larger dysfunction and bias that this instance demonstrated… We told them that not only did we expect the reinstatement of our rightful award, we also expected to see progressive policy change that would prevent this kind of 'mistake' from happening again.'

Lora DiCarlo's award was returned, policy changes were made, and the show now includes sextech in its health and wellness exhibitor category.

Still with techie things, have you ever wondered what effect spaceflight and zero gravity would have on a sex toy? Neither had I, until July 2021 when Japanese brand Tenga – best known for its intricately engineered male masturbation 'cups' – decided to find out, to help it develop future sex toys which could be used off-planet.

That was only one of the objectives of Tenga's collaboration with civilian spaceflight company Interstellar Technologies Inc, however. The others were to deliver 1,000 messages of love and freedom, and to send models of company mascots Robo and Egg Dog into space and retrieve them after they fell back to earth.

The Tenga Rocket was a 33-foot-high MOMO type, developed by Interstellar Technologies, with a 20-inch diameter, a mass of one tonne, and a maximum thrust of 12 kilonewtons. The launch took place at 17:00 JST on 31st July [National Orgasm Day! Coincidence?] at Hokkaido Spaceport in north Japan. The Tenga Rocket reached a peak altitude of 92km and views from inside the vehicle were broadcast live – a first for a commercial flight in Japan.

Data on the temperature and pressure experienced by the Tenga cup was duly recorded, helping the company achieve its aim of "becoming a pioneer in space-grade sexual devices for the new era of life in space".

If you are wondering how much this astronomical PR stunt cost, the answer might surprise you. Remember those messages of love and freedom, mentioned earlier? Well the launch cost of ¥1,833,680 (just over £12,000) was crowdfunded from 1,000 supporters paying to have their messages included in a Tenga-shaped message pod mounted on the rocket.

The result of the stunt was headlines all around the world. Google 'sex toy in space' and you will get over 60 million results, with the top listings on the coveted first page – even now, almost two years' later – devoted to Tenga's mission, from sources ranging from *interestingengineering.com* to *MailOnline*.

Finally, no chapter on PR would be complete without mentioning the impact that outrage can make, and American manufacturer Pipedream was the master of this. It took a joke category – cheap inflatable love dolls, of the sort beloved of stag parties – and used it as a sharp stick to prod celebs with.

The box artwork of its Super Star Series featured images of lookalikes dressed up as that celeb plus, for those who failed to get the connection immediately, 'hint' text. For example, the Paris doll straplines included: 'This seductive socialite gets down and dirty!' and 'I'm a filthy-rich bitch… and I mean filthy!'. And who can forget the Sarah Jessica Porkher model? Apparently, she 'loves sex in her shitty'. Other celeb-inspired dolls included Crackhead Charlie, JHO, Jessica Sin, Dirty Christina, Lindsay Fully Loaded, Finally Mylie, Kinky Kim, and J-Law, and some of the straplines really were outrageous: it was almost like the manufacturer was *inviting* legal action.

Nick Orlandino, Pipedream CEO at the time, said at the launch of J-Law: "The publicity we receive when one of these celebrity dolls hits the market is priceless," and the one that generated the most headlines was probably the Just-In Beaver in 2012. Within two days of the announcement of the doll's release, Pipedream's website experienced over two million hits and someone close to Justin Bieber was quoted by *The Sun* as saying: "Justin is absolutely incensed with this monstrosity. He's already set his lawyer on these sickos."

There was a precedent for celebs suing over products they 'inspired'. While Germany was preparing to host the FIFA World Cup in 2006, sex shop chain Beate Uhse marketed two vibrators under the names Michael B and Olli K, which some people took to be references to Germany's highest profile footballers at that time, Michael Ballack and Oliver Kahn. Even though the products were removed from sale, it was reported that a court ordered the company to pay each player €50,000 as compensation.

But I'm guessing Justin didn't set his legal attack dogs on Pipedream as the product is still listed for sale on Amazon, with reviews ranging from the one-star "Doll does not resemble the package photo. It is just a bright pink ugly man made from thin plastic" to the five-star "The doll does not look like Justin Bieber. I was ok with this and is great to have fun with". And if pop stars weren't your thing, Pipedream also took inspiration from US politics, creating Horny Hillary ('The hottest tail on the campaign trail'), Blow Up Barack ('He'll stimulate your package') and Donald Chump ('He's screwed up politics, now you can screw him back') sex dolls.

But while coverage of products like these, and the more positive 'wheezes' mentioned earlier in this chapter, undoubtedly generated exposure for the sector and helped it to grow, absolutely no one was prepared for The Great Jiggle Ball Shortage of 2012, which we'll come to next.

"It is a love story with bondage, beautiful bodies, and billionaires. It has that aspirational element as well as writing which, while being appallingly edited and flawed, does have great page-turning qualities…"

Erotic fiction has always been the most acceptable face of adult entertainment. A train traveller might quite understandably tut-tut with displeasure if a fellow passenger was watching porn on a smartphone, but eyebrows would remain firmly in place if that same passenger was reading a novel called *The Dark Desires of Deirdre Daniels*.

Erotic fiction can trace its origins back to the ancient Romans, with *The Satyricon* – believed to have been written by Petronius Arbiter – containing scenes of orgies and ritual sex, but one of the first erotic novels published in English was *Memoirs of a Woman of Pleasure*. Also known as *Fanny Hill*, it was written by John Cleland and published in 1748.

The erotic fiction genre was allowed to flourish in the 20th century after Penguin Books was charged with obscenity in 1960 for publishing an unexpurgated version of DH Lawrence's *Lady Chatterley's Lover*. The prosecution famously asked the jury if the book – which contained words such as 'fuck' and 'cunt' – was the kind "you would wish your wife or servants to read".

"Abso-bloody-lutely," replied the jury, acquitting Penguin of the charge *[Not an actual transcript of what was said in court – Ed]*.

Some mainstream publishers had their own erotic imprints as the 20th century became the 21st, under different names to distance them from their core business. Virgin Books published erotic fiction under the Nexus and Black Lace brands, for instance. Plus there were other publishers specialising in erotica including Blue Moon, Cleis Press, Silver Moon, Magic Carpet Books, Goliath, Circlet Press, the Erotic Print Society, and Taschen.

BDSM (Bondage, Discipline, Dominance, Submission, Sadism, and Masochism) was a popular theme in erotic fiction and in March 2006 I interviewed Francine Whittaker, whose latest novel *The Whipmaster* had just been published by Silver Moon.

A practising sub, Francine's literary career began with a short story being published in a Black Lace anthology called *Sugar and Spice 2*. Inspired by a holiday in Greece, when she was

– in her words – put into 'slave mode' for the entire two weeks, she began writing her first book, *The Connoisseur*.

Despite having six novels in print at the time, Francine's writing was not able to support her, reflecting the sad reality that the number of units moved in specialist literary genres was, and probably still is, a long way short of the mainstream book market.

I asked if she thought it essential that authors writing BDSM fiction should be enthusiasts for the scene, in order to write authoritatively about it, or whether it could be researched in the same way a writer would study a topic such as murder or robbery - ie without actually doing it. She replied: "There's so much information on BDSM available these days, especially via the internet, that it's certainly possible through research to write about the subject authoritatively. I know of one author, and I'm sure there are others, who work that way without ever experiencing BDSM first hand.

"But I think being an enthusiast has its advantages. Not only do I know how a crop or cane actually feels when it strikes the skin, but I know something of the conflicting emotions that go with it. I understand how a personality can change when taking on a submissive role because I feel and act differently when in 'slave' mode. Then I do things I would never consider otherwise and enjoy experiences which would seem quite absurd during my everyday life."

I also spoke to Richard Eadie from Silver Moon, Francine's publisher, about the market. He estimated that around 80% of BDSM fiction readers were men, and he had the following advice for authors: "Don't think of it as a career. Do it for fun and a useful bit of cash. That way you'll be pleasantly surprised."

He added that those who did expect to make a career out of writing erotica were probably going to be disappointed.

Lovehoney took a look at the sector in 2007 by launching an erotic writing competition, which co-founder Richard Longhurst later told me was "both brilliant and a giant pain in the arse". He explained: "We had to read all those stories. It took ages. Eventually we packaged them up as ebooks but mainly we just put them on the Lovehoney blog. It was far too time consuming."

Nevertheless, 2007 saw a new name enter the erotic fiction sector: Xcite Books. An imprint of mainstream publisher Accent Press, Xcite specialised in anthologies containing 20 themed short stories, with covers emblazoned with vivid colours, and its target market was women.

"We felt there was a need for a fresh feel to erotic writing for women," explained Hazel Cushion, managing director of Accent Press. "Our look is fun and sassy. It is time to get away from dark, whiplash covers. This range is enticing new female readers and the cover treatments mean they are suitable for front of store positioning."

Xcite's original aim was to produce 12 books a year and its first three titles – *Sex & Submission*, *Sex & Satisfaction*, and *Sex & Seduction* – let potential readers know exactly what they would find between the covers.

I caught up with Hazel in July 2009, when Xcite had moved into publishing full length novels as well as collections of short stories, and she told me, rather presciently: "Spanking is by far the most popular subject of our themed anthologies, and I do think it is an increasingly popular form of play."

Xcite was able to increase its share of the erotic fiction market when two of its rivals – Nexus and Black Lace – ceased publishing new titles following Random House's acquisition of Virgin Books. According to Hazel, Random House had just wanted Richard Branson's business books, which included *Screw It, Let's Do It*, and the two erotic imprints were thrown in as part of the deal.

Xcite titles sold for £7.99 each, with writers paid a flat fee of £50 per story for an anthology and novelists receiving 10% royalties on net receipts (more for ebooks), which seemed to confirm what Silver Moon's Richard Eadie had said earlier. It was a nice sector to be in, but no one was going to get rich from it.

Or so we thought…

The phrase 'It's the book everyone is talking about' is often bandied around inaccurately but it turned out to be true in the summer of 2012 when *Fifty Shades of Grey* appeared, seemingly from nowhere. And its success was driven almost exclusively by women. Facebook acquaintances were practically bragging about their progress, updating their status with comments like "Chapter 12!!!", and talking about the book's scenes in a remarkably candid way.

Not that many men were complaining, as *FSoG* (as I'll refer to it from now on – I don't get paid by the word, unfortunately) appeared to be responsible for stimulating their partners' interest in sex and bringing a little bit of kinkiness into the bedroom. And even if it didn't, there were other benefits for men: one told me that the summer of 2012 was the first time he had been able to watch a major football tournament in its entirety, as his wife took the book to bed early every night.

FSoG was written by English mother-of-two Erika Mitchell, using the pen name EL James. A former TV executive, *FSoG* was her first novel though she initially posted her writing online as a series of episodes set in the Twilight world under the title *Master of the Universe*.

She subsequently modified this and split it into three parts, with the first, *FSoG*, released as an ebook and print-on-demand paperback in May 2011 by an Australian self-publishing operation called The Writer's Coffee Shop Publishing House.

Part two of the trilogy, *Fifty Shades Darker*, was released in September 2011 and the final part, *Fifty Shades Freed*, followed in January 2012. Following the huge interest in the ebooks, the licence was acquired by Vintage Books and the trilogy arrived in UK bookstores in April 2012.

If you've somehow managed to avoid the whole hullabaloo, the *FSoG* saga traces the relationship between 21-year-old virgin Anastasia Steele and manipulative billionaire business tycoon Christian Grey. James said her books were 'romantic fantasy' stories, which offered women a 'holiday' from their husbands, but the rather snappier phrase chosen by the tabloids to describe them was 'mummy porn'.

As I didn't feel I was the target market for *FSoG*, I asked a female industry contact to report on it for *ETO*. She wrote: "Women are genuinely intrigued by the 'taboo' subjects in the book. I'm sure curiosity will have encouraged many to purchase it, and perhaps even see whether or not they could fit into or enjoy a Dom/Sub roleplay situation. One friend I spoke to suggested that reading an erotic novel and using her imagination was sexier than watching porn, and even more romantic."

This point was echoed by Radio 5's *Late Night Live* psychotherapist Rachel Morris who, discussing *FSoG*'s appeal, said: "Women can let themselves be turned on by written erotica in a way they often can't with visual porn. Novels like this offer guilt-free thrills, because we don't have to compare our bodies unfavourably, the way we might with a video, we can just let ourselves be carried along by the story."

Our reviewer continued: "The main character, Ana Steele, comes across as very naïve, which I am sure was the author's intention, allowing us to follow her journey through the trilogy. However, the book is quite repetitive and the whole area of Dom and Sub could have been explored in more depth. It was a very tame introduction into this area of sexuality, more childish than erotic at some points, mainly down to the actual language being used. And I think Ana would be a regular visitor at her local A&E due to the number of times she bit down on her bottom lip, a look that drove Christian wild with passion apparently."

Whatever its literary merits, or shortcomings, *FSoG* became the fastest selling paperback of all time and in June 2012 the trilogy was estimated to have captured 25% of the adult fiction market, occupying the top three slots in *The Sunday Times* bestselling paperback fiction charts.

Book industry insiders said it was highly unusual for any title from a previously unknown author to sell in decent numbers, unless it was a film adaptation, but the hype surrounding *FSoG* came from word of mouth and social media, and its sales were driven by people who didn't typically buy books on a regular basis.

It was a great story for the mainstream media – saucy fan fiction-derived erotica by middle-aged mother of two etc – and it fed on its own success, with its subsequent record-breaking sales getting it even more exposure.

I asked Xcite's Hazel Cushion if *FSoG*'s success had irked her and she replied: "No, I welcome it with open arms because it proves that there is a demand for erotic fiction, and it is helping it become mainstream. Now you can walk into your local supermarket and buy *Fifty Shades of Grey*. That is fairly revolutionary and bodes well for the future. It has reached a far wider audience and, now their appetites have been whetted, they will be hungry for more."

Discussing the reasons behind its success Hazel said: "Basically it is a love story with bondage, beautiful bodies, and billionaires. It has that aspirational element as well as writing which, while being appallingly edited and flawed, does have great page-turning qualities… [but] I also felt that it was implied that his dominant desires were a result of his damaged childhood. I think a great many people who enjoy consensual BDSM play would take issue with that."

Hazel added that several of her company's books had enjoyed significant sales spikes since the publication of *FSoG*, and that other publishers were "dashing around trying to scoop up new erotic titles" within the book trade.

Tabloids were quick to publish 'If you liked that, you'll love this…' features which highlighted other BDSM fiction, but it wasn't just booksellers who were profiting from Fifty Shades Fever. By putting BDSM activities and products firmly into the mainstream, EL James was sending a whole new set of customers into the arms of retailers who sold floggers, whips, and jiggle balls.

Writing in the August 2012 issue of *ETO*, Katie Byrne, Ann Summers' PR and social media manager, reported: "Our sales figures continue to increase week on week and the demand has never been so feverish. The consumer has been swept up in the hysteria of curiosity and that ever present 'fear of missing out'.

"At least two or three times a week I am told by women that they are reading the book 'because everybody else is' or 'so many people are talking about it, I am not privy to these secret, illicit conversations' or better still entries via Facebook that read 'off to bed with a glass of wine and to curl up with Mr Grey'…

"As a business, we have not seen anything like this in our 30 plus years in the industry; it is one thing stocking the product, but quite another when demand steamrolls supplies."

Items namechecked in the books were flying off the shelves, particularly jiggle balls (also known as Kegel balls, love balls, sex balls, pleasure balls, and Ben Wa balls): so much so that almost every supplier in Europe was out of stock at one point.

Ah, what tales we'll tell when our grandchildren ask, "What was it like during The Great Jiggle Ball Shortage of 2012?"

One retailer told me at the time: "Sales of our sex balls have increased by over 1,000%. Sales are so strong that customers have demanded that we stock an array of different ones. Everything we get vanishes before we have time to breathe."

As mentioned earlier in the chapter on online retail, my 2012 visit to Bondara coincided with the height of Fifty Shades Fever and boss Chris Simms told me: "It has increased our business 100% compared to 12 months ago. That's across the board."

Fifty Shades Fever also brought other opportunities. London retailer Sh! held a 'BDSM in the Bedroom' workshop at its Hoxton Square branch, hosted by one of London's professional Mistresses. For £25 a ticket, guests – women only – were initiated into the timeless methods and skills used by Mistresses to govern the desire and sexual arousal of others.

But it wasn't all fun and games. By the end of July, the London Fire Brigade reported that it had been called out to 79 instances of people being trapped in handcuffs.

On the back of the books' success, trade magazine *The Bookseller* reported that Simon & Schuster would be publishing Rebecca Chance's *Naughty Bits*, a collection of the romance author's scenes from earlier novels which were previously considered 'too hot to print', and that publisher Orion had paid a six-figure sum for UK and Commonwealth rights for the Eighty Days erotic trilogy written by Vina Jackson. The first title, *Eighty Days Yellow*, was set to be published on 19th July in paperback and ebook, followed by *Eighty Days Blue* and *Eighty Days Red* later in the year.

Other mainstream publishers were also getting in on the act: Pan Macmillan released Eve Sinclair's *Jane Eyre Laid Bare*, a rewritten version of Charlotte Bronte's classic featuring the erotic reimagining of the relationship between the young governess and her employer, Edward Rochester. Oh, and look over there: is that Black Lace coming out of retirement?

Discussing Fifty Shades Fever in the August 2012 issue of *ETO*, author and journalist Emily Dubberley wrote: "Book publishers are obviously wading through a slushpile of erotica, desperate to find the next *FSoG*. New titles, reprints, and fast-turnaround production has led to homages and parodies in equal measure, but it's not just the obvious product sectors that are booming. You can buy *FSoG* CDs featuring the music from the book, you can go on a *FSoG* holiday to Portland, Seattle, or San Francisco, with Pinot Gris, helicopter rides, and, at Personality Hotels, you can have an 'intimacy kit' that includes a vibrator and feathers, that is 'meant to unleash your creative shades of Grey'.

"You can also find recipes on *cafemom.com* for *FSoG*-inspired cocktails including Kinky Fuckery on the Rocks, The Red Room of Pain, and The Twitchy Palm, and you can even get a *FSoG* curry at Michelin-listed Indian fine dining venue, The Ambrette, which is serving a special six-course sampler menu priced at £39.99, using ingredients reputed to have strong aphrodisiac qualities."

Not content with reporting record sales, brands which specialised in 'soft bondage' items, particularly Sex & Mischief and Pipedream, cashed in further.

Sex & Mischief rush-released a brand-new product that would have been unthinkable the previous year: a gent's tie. In grey, obviously, it was aimed at those who wanted their bondage sessions to be as close to the book as possible.

Fellow US manufacturer Pipedream created 'limited editions' of a host of its Fetish Fantasy Series products, with boxes that had artwork remarkably similar in style and colour to the trilogy's covers.

A representative from Pipedream's UK distributor explained knowingly: "This range has taken some of the best pieces from the Fetish Fantasy Series and given the boxes a whole new splash of colour, albeit a few shades darker than before. This will really appeal to people who may be new to sex toys or may have recently been inspired by books or films to give the light side of S&M a try. There are 31 products that have been given a facelift, from crops and paddles to Ben Wa balls and ball gags, and the range is almost fifty times more eye-catching when displayed together. We do expect these items to sell really well, so it will be a grey day for those who miss out on this great range."

The world's largest trade show for the literary industry, Frankfurt Book Fair (281,753 visitors and more than 7,300 exhibitors from 100 countries in 2012) was staged in October and publishers were reportedly 'flooded with erotica' in the wake of the global success of *FSoG*. David Shelley, publisher at Little Brown, was quoted in *The Guardian* as saying: "We've seen loads of erotica on offer – Scandinavian erotica, Japanese erotica, every sort", while Faber & Faber's Lee Brackstone heard about "tonnes" of erotica, "the latest being apparently zombie erotica".

S.E.C.R.E.T, a novel by LM Adeline featuring a young woman who joins a secret society to liberate her sexual self, reportedly sold for a high six-figure sum in America while

Virago announced the 'antidote' to *FSoG: Fifty Shades of Feminism*, which featured the stories of 50 women reflecting on 'the shades that inspired them and what being a woman means to them today'.

The temperature was rising and the fever got higher in November 2012 when Lovehoney announced it had developed, in association with *FSoG* author EL James, an 'official' Fifty Shades of Grey Pleasure Products Collection. Consisting of nine sex toys and 11 soft bondage accessories, the products had names inspired by passages from the books, so consumers could buy items like Inner Goddess Silver Pleasure Balls and You Are Mine Metal Handcuffs.

Although Lovehoney allowed European retailers to carry products it had developed in-house, it had previously kept them all to itself in the UK. But this initiative saw the firm establishing a B2B arm to supply its rivals, along with any mainstream retailer who wished to jump on the bandwagon. And jump onboard they did. The first batch of products – encompassing a staggering half a million units – sold out straight away, leaving some retailers disappointed, but hey, there was always Valentine's Day to look forward to...

"We plan to be able to supply all UK retailers with our iconic new brand to bring thousands of new customers into UK adult stores for Valentine's Day," said a spokesperson. "Our vision is to use the *FSoG* brand to bring millions of new customers into the pleasure industry, not just throughout the *FSoG* phenomenon but for the next ten years and beyond. We want to encourage new customers who've never visited a pleasure retailer into stores and ensure they have a great first experience of our rapid developing industry."

The spokesperson got a bit carried away though, adding: "When introducing the *FSoG* collection, we suggest that you talk to each customer about what chapters and scenes they loved best and then help them select their own collection of four or five items, to let their fantasies become a reality and give them their perfect *FSoG* experience."

Writing in the December 2012 issue of *ETO*, Nigel Hughson, from 'serious' BDSM manufacturer House of Eros, wasn't exactly counting down the days until he could buy an 'official' product as he was no fan of the existing lines that retailers were selling in huge numbers: "I recently ventured into a high street store and had a good look at a faux leather flogger hanging on display," he wrote. "Unfortunately, when I felt the plastic falls, they actually cut my finger.

"Christian Grey, as a multi-millionaire with his private helicopter, jet set lifestyle, and penchant for buying his girlfriend the odd Audi, would hardly be seen using a faux leather offering. Given his experience, albeit fictional, he without a doubt would have used real leather.

It is all too easy to throw at the public a range of products that are cheap to produce and, at the base level, have some function, but in reality many of these products would be dismissed with contempt by the BDSM community. No player would be seen waving a handful of faux leather at a club for fear of being laughed out of the door."

He went on to warn: "The question we as an industry have to consider is, are we in danger of letting this upturn in interest in the BDSM lifestyle market pass us by? Cheap plastic products will only result in disappointed customers but by offering them good quality, authentic products we should be able to take full advantage of this wonderful opportunity."

Also writing in the December issue of *ETO*, Ann Summers' brand copywriter Stuart Nugent predicted that, post-*FSoG*, the UK industry would never be the same again: "We're facing a new sexual epoch," he stated, in a piece that could have been an audition for a political speechwriter's role. "An age fuelled by the mainstreaming of the previously subversive, an age that counters the counterculture, an age that quells the excitement of kinkiness by making it ordinary. Vanilla, perhaps, is the new kinky, and simply keeping up with this quiet revolution is no longer enough. To survive, and to continue to grow, we need to be ahead of the curve that's ahead of the curve."

He added: "*FSoG* has opened up a nationwide conversation about sex, in a way that I've never seen happen before. The general population has become more sexually literate over the last year, the envelope of sexual propriety has been broadened, discussion of sex and sexuality is more articulate, our customers are savvier than ever and BDSM is being discussed everywhere, from coffee mornings to cocktail suppers, from school runs to train commutes, up and down the country."

As you can tell, Stuart was, and still is, a fine wordsmith. He's no longer at Ann Summers but he's recently published a book called *Just Crazy Enough to Work*, which you might enjoy.

As 2012 became 2013, the *FSoG* juggernaut continued to bludgeon its way through sales records, and in June the Fifty Shades of Grey Official Sensual Care Collection joined the Official Pleasure Products Collection. The nine new products, which included sensual bath and massage oils, were also named after passages in the book, and said to be infused with Christian Grey's signature scent of bergamot, sandalwood, and musk.

Lovehoney's Neal Slateford said at the launch: "The aim is to distil the extraordinary sexual chemistry enjoyed by Christian and Ana and capture it in a bottle. We have worked very closely with EL James to perfectly blend the oils and aromas she had in mind when she created Ana and Christian."

And in August came the *FSoG* lingerie and underwear ranges via BlueBella. It included a men's cotton Christian Grey boxer, a trio of panty gift sets featuring some of the book's most memorable catchphrases, embroidered frill ribbon tie briefs, baby doll sets, and detailed lace button-up briefs alongside multi-use body bows and open bra and brief sets with detachable silk satin ties.

But while those profiting from it were obviously delighted that its reach continued to extend into every conceivable product sector, signs of Fifty Shades Fatigue could be seen in some areas of the trade.

And even those who I thought would benefit the most from *FSoG*'s popularity, the established specialist writers of BDSM and erotic fiction, were less than enthused when I brought up the subject. I chatted with two – KD Grace and Kay Jaybee – at the grand opening of a new adult store, where the authors were reading extracts from their books, in the summer of 2013.

"When *FSoG* came out we were really hopeful," Kay told me. "It was mainstream, it was everywhere, and we thought people would read it, enjoy it, and hopefully they'd find us. And for about three months that was exactly what happened. We were both getting emails from readers who had discovered us after buying *FSoG*, saying our books were much hotter etc. It was great. There was an upsurge in sales, particularly for BDSM and heavier kink books. But it took a few months for people to twig that *FSoG* wasn't actually BDSM, it was erotic romance. You could read the first third and have no idea there was any sex in the book."

KD added: "I read it to see what she had done right, because obviously she had done something right and maybe it was something the rest of us could learn from. I believe it was about page 95 before there was any sex. I think it got so much coverage because the sex that was included was a little bit kinky."

"There's no real substance to that side of the story," Kay said, "which is what you would expect if you were buying an erotic book."

But their real problem with *FSoG* was what it led to: so many people thought 'An ordinary woman wrote this book and made lots of money – I could do that'.

"There were two elements to it," explained KD. "They knew she was not a writer and so there was a huge rise in self-publishing. You didn't have to go through an agent or a publisher, you just had to follow Amazon's step-by-step instructions and then you were in. So there was this huge surge of stuff that would never normally have crossed a publisher's doorstep...

"The second element was the big publishers decided that they needed to get on this bandwagon. They looked at *FSoG* as a formula, so all they were interested in was billionaire and virgin combinations. How many ways can you do billionaire and virgin? There was even one about an alien vampire billionaire and a virgin. But that was what publishers wanted. That was all they wanted."

Kay concluded sadly: "We all expected people to explore other erotic fiction, but it seems they just want the same thing but packaged in a different way."

Not much had changed by 2014, when I spoke to representatives from several publishers of erotica for an *ETO* feature on the state of the market. One of the largest, Cleis Press, actually reported sales on Amazon had declined by almost 20% the previous year due to what was referred to as 'fifty shades of imitation'.

And although all were still wedded to the concept of printing physical books, the popularity of ebooks had led to changes in their business models. One had switched to a print-on-demand system, and another was making its entire catalogue available digitally on a subscription basis. And when I broached the subject of *FSoG*, and its impact on other publishers of erotica, there were some interesting comments.

Brenda Knight of Cleis Press said her company was still feeling the effects of *FSoG*, both good and bad: "The downside is the thousands and thousands of self-published erotica titles," she said. "This resulted in an absolute saturation of the market. Where Cleis Press had dominated – pun intended – the submissive market, we were now jockeying against both well-known authors and first-time self-published authors who decided to upload their barely edited books.

"Many found that they did not achieve EL James levels of recognition, and started downpricing their books to $0.99, $0.50, or free. We always believe that quality will win out, high standards will win the day, and we're standing on the banks, waiting for the waters of the erotica tsunami to recede. But ultimately, if it got more people reading erotica and opened minds, we're happy about that and see it as a good thing."

This sentiment was echoed by Hazel Cushion of Xcite Books, who said: "It was positive because it got erotica off the top shelf and onto the supermarket shelf but negative because it suddenly became a very saturated market. Every publisher dusted off their erotic backlist or created a new one and every Tom, Dick, and Harry self-published too. There was no quality control and people looking for a similar read to *FSoG* often got put off the genre because the next book they bought was either far more extreme or an unedited, self-published first attempt at erotica."

But anyone hoping that Fifty Shades Fever would be over by 2015 would be very disappointed, as we'll see…

"We've had people travelling to Brighton just to come to the shops to meet us. I never thought that I'd ever have people asking to have a selfie taken with me holding a dildo."

I worked in a small supermarket in the 1980s and we would always know what had been advertised on prime-time television the night before, because it sold out pretty quickly the next day.

Costs, not to mention broadcasting regulations, meant mainstream television advertising was not an option for most sellers of sex toys in the early noughties. But they still occasionally popped their perky little heads up.

I honestly don't know when the first sex toy appeared on TV screens, but a 1998 episode of HBO's *Sex and the City*, entitled 'The Turtle and the Hare', is generally credited with being the first to introduce a rabbit vibrator to a mainstream global audience. If you've never seen the episode, Charlotte, after borrowing Miranda's vibrator (a Vibratex Rabbit Pearl), decides that staying in is the new going out.

The broadcasting of this episode reportedly resulted in demand for rabbit vibes reaching unprecedented levels, and despite significant advancements in sex toy design over the last quarter of a century, variations on the rabbit theme are still popular today.

Sex toys appeared on UK TV several times in the early noughties in programmes like *More Sex Tips for Girls* (Channel 4) and *Am I Good In Bed?* (ITV) and there were high hopes for *Sex on the Settee* (Channel 5). This latter series was scheduled to begin its run on 12th August 2004 and was billed as '*Sex and the City* comes to life'. It was said to feature a group of women discussing their sex lives and reporting on three sex toys, all while quaffing champagne. It sounded quite the hoot.

Dominic Hawes, MD of Mantric, a company that supplied some of the products for the series, told me at the time: "There is nothing quite like television coverage to boost sales of sex toys… [This show] presents a huge opportunity for shop and website owners because people are going to be asking for products by name, and that rarely happens in this industry."

Unfortunately, *Sex on the Settee* got bumped, supposedly due to the opening ceremony of the 2004 Athens Olympics, and I still don't know if it was ever broadcast. Searching for it on Google now only brings up results which I'd rather not have in my browsing history.

The most likely place to see sex toys on television at this time was on post-watershed chat shows, when episodes with less than scintillating guests could be brought to life by the introduction of a mystery gadget: "What do you think this is for, ladies and gentlemen?"

A good example would be the VibraExciter, a device with a name which could have been coined by Mike Myers: "One book, *Swedish-made VibraExciters And Me: (This Sort of Thing Is My Bag Baby)*, by Austin Powers…"

The VibraExciter was actually rather neat. Its compact form and silver colour resembled the Samsung A300 flip phone, which all the cool kids had at the time. It differed by having a bullet vibrator the size of a tablet – the type you ingest, not play games on – attached to it by a cable. The VibraExciter detected incoming calls on any mobile phone close by and would stimulate the bullet until the call ended. It could also be triggered by an incoming text message or, for traditionalists, it could be controlled manually.

BBC 1's *Friday Night with Jonathan Ross*, which aired on 3rd December 2004, saw the host demonstrate the VibraExciter to his audience, who thought the bullet vibe dancing on his desk was absolutely hilarious.

Around the same time, Channel 4 and E4 broadcast a reality TV show that sounds ripe for reviving, given the popularity of *Love Island*. Made by Big Brother producer Edemol, *Fool Around… with my Girlfriend* saw a single boy live with four girls for a week. They all claimed to be single but only one of them was telling the truth: the others had their boyfriends living right next door, watching their every move. If the guy figured out who the single girl was, the pair of them won £10,000. If he picked someone who was already spoken for, she – and her boyfriend – got the cash.

The show's boudoir contained lingerie, massage oils, and erotic games supplied by Lovehoney, and the firm's Neal Slateford commented: "Endemol wanted to team up with a leading company that stocks a wide range of quality products, which made Lovehoney the natural choice. Lovehoney will be linked from the Channel 4 website, so it was also important for them to have a partner who could guarantee first class customer service, and once again Lovehoney fits the bill perfectly."

December 2005 saw Jonathan Ross titillating his audience again, this time with a Vibrating Space Hopper – which was exactly what it sounded like – and the following June he introduced them to The Cone. He spent several minutes talking about this non-phallic vibe, even suggesting that ladies could amuse themselves with it while the FIFA World Cup was on. He added that it had 16 programmes – "more than Channel 5" – and a giant screen showed viewers three of the suggested positions they could adopt to enjoy the device.

Another gadget that benefited from a Ross review was the iBuzz Two, which 'converted' music into vibrations, in December 2006. "I have found the perfect present for couples who like sex and music – it's called the iBuzz," said Ross as he plugged the device into his iPod. "It's perfect for couples because she gets an earth-shattering orgasm and the man gets to be the DJ. That's just about the perfect evening, isn't it?"

It probably won't surprise you to learn that Lovehoney's PR machine was responsible for the iBuzz getting on the show, just as it was for putting a Sqweel into the hands of Philip Schofield on ITV's *This Morning* in 2010. That same year a dildo popped up in an episode of *Peep Show*, when Mark – worrying if he could satisfy Dobby in bed – purchased one to lend him a hand, should he need it. But perhaps the most impactful appearance by a sex toy on any mainstream television programme was a 2012 episode of Channel 4's *10 o'clock Live* show, when co-host Charlie Brooker introduced viewers to a Fuck Me Silly 3 Mega Masturbator.

If you don't know the product – and frankly I'd be a little surprised if you did – it's made by US manufacturer Pipedream and it's essentially a life-size lower torso of a female lying on her stomach. So it's got feet, legs, a bum, and a vagina, but that's all. It's like she was in the process of nakedly sliding through a hole in the floor to the level below, when the hole sealed up around her.

Brooker was performing a piece to camera about a woman called Samantha Brick, who made headlines all over the world after she wrote an article for the *Daily Mail* stating that women hated her because she was so beautiful. Brick claimed that other women were scared their husbands would want to have sex with her and Brooker agreed with her – but only because, he said, men will have sex with almost anything. He added: "If you don't believe me take a look at these genuine sex aids for men we bought today."

Brooker then produced a "tinned anus" and the boxed Pipedream torso, to hoots of laughter from the studio audience. Judging by the ease with which he placed it down in front of him, I would guess the Pipedream box was empty as the product itself, made from soft TPR material, weighs over 20lb.

"It costs over £400," Brooker said. "And it says on the back, 'you've always dreamt of fucking a long-legged beauty like this'. They know me so well! I have! But in my dream she had a head."

Less risqué, but probably reaching a far bigger audience, ITV's *This Morning* magazine show, often featuring Phillip Schofield and Holly Willoughby, occasionally adds sex toys to its mix of fashion, cooking, and health advice. One particularly memorable episode aired on 25th May 2016, where Phil and Holly and guest Tracey Cox were discussing the recently published issue of *Good Housekeeping,* which included sex toys in its Tried & Tested section, and a survey of 1,000 women which revealed that 42% owned a vibrator.

Tracey, a sex and relationships expert who has a branded range of sex toys and lubricants exclusively sold through Lovehoney, played the role of industry cheerleader admirably, revealing that the worldwide sex toy market was worth $15 billion and was set to rise to $52 billion by 2020 – though no source for these figures was cited. She went on to inform viewers "You're considered odd if you *don't* have a vibrator these days".

Tracey also did her bit for Lovehoney. When discussing its Desire Clitoral Vibrator, which was the *Good Housekeeping* panel's favourite toy, she told Phil and Holly: "Lovehoney is an amazing company because they offer a money-back guarantee for one year. If you don't like something you can just send it back."

The company got another sneaky plug when Tracey was talking about the Ann Summers Love Heart: Tracey referred to it as a Lovehoney product, before correcting herself.

Incidentally, the Fuck Me Silly 3 Mega Masturbator that Charlie Brooker was showcasing earlier also popped up in episode three of the FXX comedy *Dave* in April 2020. The episode revolved around Dave's obsession with his secret 'lover', the Fuck Me Silly 3. Pipedream reported that the product received an immediate boost in internet searches and customer demand, claiming its appearance "moves American culture one step closer towards the normalisation of sex toys for men."

In addition to providing titillation for chat show audiences, and making cameo appearances as the comedy love interest, TV bosses realised there was a more interesting tale to tell about sex toys: the business of selling them.

One of the first programmes to cover this was a 2011 episode of Channel 4's *Undercover Boss.* The format saw senior executives working 'undercover' in relatively low positions in their own companies, in order to find out how the businesses can be improved. They were accompanied by a film crew which, employees were told, was making a documentary about entry-level workers in that sector.

If it sounds dull, it wasn't, especially when the incognito boss revealed themselves at the end, rewarding staff who had impressed them and providing additional training to those in need of it – even if, secretly, the bosses might have preferred to give them their P45s.

The first episode of series three saw the *Undercover Boss* cameras follow Vanessa Gold, deputy managing director of Ann Summers (and sister of CEO Jacqueline, who was, viewers were told, 'too famous' to be convincing in an undercover role) as she worked on the shop floor of several of the chain's branches.

Even without the wig and glasses used to disguise Vanessa, I doubt any of the staff she met would have guessed she had spent several decades working within the Ann Summers organisation, particularly when it came to dealing with customers on the shop floor. Vanessa appeared to be quite reserved compared to her staff, who came across as confident and enthusiastic women who loved their jobs.

This resulted in a rather inverted version of the *Undercover Boss* format, where the boss is normally the star. Here Vanessa travelled between the Blackburn, Exeter, and Bristol branches of Ann Summers almost like a Louis Theroux figure. By the end of the programme we had learned intimate details about the lives of the staff (and even some customers) but we knew little about Vanessa other than she was married to a policeman, had a penchant for expensive shoes, and had never worked in a shop before.

Part of the appeal of this type of programme is the insider information we discover about the sector being featured, but few trade secrets were revealed other than Ann Summers party planners were required to pay £3.50 a week to rent their standard samples kit, they had to buy additional items themselves to keep their stock fresh, and they earned 23% commission on sales.

The sales staff had no real gripes and very few cuts would have been required for the programme to be used in a recruitment campaign, suggesting that Ann Summers was a pretty sweet place to work. Viewers agreed, as the company reported record levels of recruitment enquiries after the show was broadcast.

Ann Summers was back on our screens in September 2011 via a brand partnership with ITV2 which included the first ever TV campaign for the chain. The retailer and the broadcaster co-hosted dual-branded roadshows at key regional shopping malls in Birmingham, London, Manchester, and Essex in a quest to find the UK's sexiest face. The best 20 faces were scheduled to be filmed for a two-minute advert to be broadcast during the final episode of ITV2's *The Only Way Is Essex*, with the public being asked to vote for their favourite.

Sex toys returned to Channel 4 in May of the following year when the documentary *More Sex Please We're British* was broadcast. The programme went behind the scenes of Lovehoney and followed the firm's progress as it attempted to revamp upmarket Covent Garden boutique Coco de Mer, which it had acquired in 2011 from founder Sam Roddick, and prepare for Valentine's Day, its busiest time of the year.

The broadcast reportedly brought in a deluge of new business: so much so that Lovehoney's website crashed during transmission. This had a knock-on effect with some other online retailers, whose servers also crashed due to the volume of traffic they were receiving from customers unable to visit Lovehoney.

June 2013 saw Channel 4 take a look at the journey sex toys take from initial idea to finished product – from brain fart to shopping cart, as I headlined a similar article in *ETO* – in *Sex Toy Stories*, another fly-on-the-wall documentary. The hook to hang the programme on was a search conducted by Ann Summers for 'real women' to help design a new range of sex toys. It sounds contrived – and it was, obviously – but it would have also been quite an eye-opener for anyone unfamiliar with the sector.

The narrator explained that over half the women in the UK have used a vibrator but most are designed by men. After a short pause, presumably so viewers could shout 'Boo! Smash the patriarchy!', we were told that us viewers would be following a "radical experiment" which would result in a vibrator designed by women for women.

I felt that calling this concept "radical" was a bit disingenuous. I could have reeled off the names of many women who were involved in the creative process at other companies at this time.

Like a cut scene from *The Apprentice*, the camera followed Ann Summers CEO Jacqueline Gold walking purposefully into a boardroom, where she spoke about potential competitors. "Company profits were down last year," our narrator explained, and threw in a quick double-entendre. "But Jacqueline has a unique idea to stay on top."

We moved on to the recruiting process. The eight chosen women were given a snappy collective name – The O Team – and, like Simon Cowell putting together a vocal group in *The X Factor*, there was a suspicion that some had been chosen to fit specific roles. Here was a shy 22-year-old virgin who had never used a sex toy before, there was a 47-year-old woman who could not reach orgasm, and don't forget the 70-year-old straight-talking great-grandmother. Simon Cowell would have adored her.

As stipulated in *The Bumper Book of Constructed Reality TV Show Cliches*, the narrator then introduced a sense of peril to the proceedings: "The toy has to be on the shelves before next Valentine's Day, so they have less than a year to turn their ideas into reality."

Ann Summers senior buyer Mark Brewer met the women and asked them to each come up with an idea. They were shown some vintage vibes for inspiration and also given samples of current products to test, so they could appreciate what they were up against.

There then followed the only scene in the programme which could have generated an OFCOM complaint: a woman was 'running errands' (as real women do) while wearing a remote-control vibe in her undies. She was describing the sensation while she was driving, implying that she was wearing it and it was turned on. While driving? Really? We followed her into a supermarket and – oh no! – she's lost the controller and can't turn it off! What's that you're saying, Jolly Green Giant? Even you think this scene is too corny?

The programme ended with a head and shoulders to-camera shot of a bubbly young woman urging viewers: "If you haven't used a sex toy before, seriously, go out there get yourself one and try it and you'll never go back to not using them again."

While some industry insiders thought the programme came across as an Ann Summers advertorial, it also touched on some sensitive issues and treated the participants respectfully. There was no sniggering at the products or the people who make, sell, and buy them. If, as stated, half the women in the UK had used a vibe, the programme might well have tempted some of the other half to give one a go.

One of the stars of *Sex Toy Stories*, Ann Summers senior buyer Mark Brewer, wrote in the following month's issue of *ETO*: "In the immediate aftermath of the documentary airing, we saw website traffic rise to double our previous record number of visitors at any one time. The Twittersphere had a similar response and we saw almost a 20% increase in followers in the few days that followed. It certainly seemed that whatever your opinion, whether you enjoyed the documentary or not, the subject of sex really does get the nation talking.

"Perhaps the most surprising thing about the show, however, is the fact that the overwhelming majority of people who watched it weren't shocked by it. Conversation across social media was around the women and the products, rather than outrage at the subject matter. It could have been a documentary about a group of women designing something as ordinary as fridges, which demonstrates how natural the language of sex is becoming... *Sex Toy Stories* was much more than a show about sex toy design, it represents the fact that the UK is ready to talk about sex like never before."

Lovehoney looked on with interest. You want behind the scenes? We'll give you behind the scenes. And they did the following year with *Frisky Business*. Debuting in March 2014, this documentary had six episodes, each of which focused on different areas of the business and the staff in charge of them. Developed by the same production company that had previously brought Lovehoney into living rooms with *More Sex Please*, Bristol-based Oblong, *Frisky Business* was broadcast on the Lifetime channel.

As Lifetime could only be received by Sky and Virgin subscribers, viewing figures were likely to have been significantly less than the previous documentaries but the series was sold to several overseas broadcasters and hey – take a wild guess at which Bath-based business was not only looking to dominate the UK but also had ambitions to become a global player?

Lovehoney already had offices in America, Australia, and Germany and it was about to open one in France. But, while conceding that the programme was a pretty good way to introduce the business to a worldwide audience, co-founder Richard Longhurst was also quick to warn of the potential pitfalls any rivals seeking to emulate Lovehoney's initiative would face: "Making a TV series is not easy," he said. "You have to provide engaging content for the cameras, which means that your staff need to be wholly on board with the whole project... You also have to remember that the cameras may carry on rolling when you don't want them to. Anyone embarking on a project like this needs to do it with their eyes wide open."

As mentioned in the earlier chapter focusing on Ann Summers, sex toys channel-hopped to ITV in 2016 via the six-part dramady, *Brief Encounters*. Based on Jacqueline Gold's 1995 memoir, *Good Vibrations: The True Story of Ann Summers*, it followed the fictionalised fortunes of four Ann Summers' agents in the 1980s.

If I'm honest, my expectations for the programme were low. The pun in the title was a bit stale and, besides, it was on ITV, the channel that had recently brought us a game show based on an end-of-the-pier coin-pushing machine (*Tipping Point*). But, out of a resigned sense of duty, I was watching at 9:00pm on 4th July when the first episode aired.

I actually enjoyed it and thought it would be good exposure for Ann Summers, not just at the time but for years to come, as all original programming seems to be either repeated many times or sold on to streaming platforms.

And as is often the case with Ann Summers' initiatives, I also thought it would be beneficial for other businesses that dealt in adult products. While the focus was on empowering women, there was a clear 'sex toys are non-threatening and a fun thing to get involved with' undercurrent running throughout the programme.

Television critics' reaction to the first episode was generally favourable. *The Guardian* said: "It's fun. Just good enough to while away an hour without making you want to throw something at the screen (though I came perilously close when the Common Girl from the Salon mistook Pauline's potpourri for nibbles), and just bad enough to make your eyes mist with longing for the great days of *Making Out, Clocking Off, Playing The Field...*"

The Telegraph said it was: "An unpromising pitch on paper, perhaps, but this first episode was a revelation: frank, funny, and full of heart... It was as if Victoria Wood had rewritten *The Full Monty*. *Brief Encounters* was drama by women, about women – but not just for women."

And *The Times* said: "As a depiction of a very British sexual revolution, it was as soapy as scented bubble bath, as light as gossamer knickers, and, like a 1982 playlist on shuffle, the era-reminding hits kept on coming."

Despite healthy viewing figures of around five million, *Brief Encounters'* time on our screens was sadly all too brief, and ITV did not commission a second series. Ah well, I'm sure there is someone currently beavering away on a similar dramedy about the early days of the Lovehoney founders. And if there isn't, I might do it myself.

With the UK industry's two biggest names now familiar to viewers, TV production companies began scouting for other stories to tell about the sex toys sector, and Channel 4 found an intriguing one in 2019. *A Very British Sex Shop* took viewers behind the scenes again but this time it focused on the Richardson family, who owned Brighton adult stores Taboo and Lust. Tim Richardson had been running the shops for over two decades and did so with his current wife Calandra and his ex-wife Nancy, mother to Tim's two children, who Tim wanted to eventually take over the business.

Yes, that does sound like the recipe for a long-running sitcom, and it had its moments. Elaine Hackett, creative director at producers Crackit Productions, commented: "Crackit loves to find and deliver rare access that offers humour alongside little known revelations. That's exactly what this eye-opening film does, going behind the often-intimidating window of the sex shop. The Richardsons, their team, and their customers are funny, warm, and honest, offering us a view into a world that many of us are intrigued by, but very rarely see."

After the broadcast, star Tim Richardson told me: "It could have backfired but it's done us a huge amount of good. It's really incredible what one show on Channel 4 can do for your business. We've had people travelling to Brighton just to come to the shops to meet us. I never thought that I'd ever have people asking to have a selfie taken with me holding a dildo."

This wasn't the first time the Taboo store had been seen on screen. In the summer of 2006, it was featured throughout the second series of *Sugar Rush*, Julie Burchill's teen lesbian drama. Set in Brighton, the shop – renamed The Munch Box for TV – was owned by the main character's girlfriend in the series.

Bolton store Softy's Hard Stuff was a pioneer in this area, popping up in two Peter Kay shows. It appears in an episode called 'The Ice Cream Man Cometh' of *That Peter Kay Thing*, a series first broadcast in early 2000, and it was also used in a deleted scene from series two of *Phoenix Nights* (the scene can be found in the extras section of the DVD). And the Watford branch of Simply Pleasure starred in an episode of *Little Britain* with Matt Lucas in 2006, though the name of the store was changed to De Sex Winkel, as the scene was set in Belgium.

Sex toys were back on our screens in November 2019, courtesy of Channel 5 offshoot 5 Star. *Inside The Sex Toy Factory* visited vibrating wand specialists Doxy, Lovehoney, and dildo maker Godemiche, and representatives from all three companies spoke about the industry and their latest launches. Also appearing in the programme was a Dorset potter who made ceramic dildos, and she was seen presenting her wares to Brighton retailers She Said and Taboo.

The programme culminated with the three featured toys being discussed by a panel, which was described as "the UK's leading sex toy industry influencers". Narrated in a knowing style by comedian Jess Fostekew, my only criticism of the programme was that it tried to cover too much ground in a single one-hour episode. I can definitely see a market for a 'Dragons' Den for sex toys', should someone wish to expand that aspect of the show.

The first sex toy to be advertised on a terrestrial television channel in the UK was the Durex Play Vibrations, which popped up on both Channel 4 and Channel 5 on 24th November 2006. Broadcasting restrictions meant the 30-second ad for the disposable vibrating cock ring could only be shown after 11.00pm but it was worth waiting up for. A couple were sat at a dinner table and the man handed the woman a ring box. She opened it and eagerly accepted his proposal. You know what that ring was, don't you?

You'd think Durex MD Martyn Ward would have been happy at making history in this way, but he commented, rather tetchily: "We firmly believe that the post-11 o'clock restriction is too severe for Durex Play Vibrations, and we will be doing everything we can to reduce the watershed to after 9pm instead. There is nothing rude or crude about the advert, which is tastefully shot, and we feel this restriction is hypercritical, given the images of a sexual nature you quite regularly see on TV at this time of night."

And so it came to pass that, in addition to trading blows via the medium of documentaries, the next battleground for Ann Summers and Lovehoney became the gaps between the programmes. In the run up to Christmas 2012, Ann Summers launched its biggest TV campaign to date, tagged 'Christmas For Grown Ups'. There were three versions of the ad: a 20-second cut, a slightly raunchier 30-second cut for later in the evening, and then an uncensored cut for online.

Have yourself a sex toy little Christmas? Not exactly. Ann Summers brand copyrighter Stuart Nugent explained the campaign's premise in *ETO*: "We wanted to say that there is space for intimacy at Christmas alongside all the other traditions and conventions, that the two things – Christmas and intimacy – are not mutually exclusive. The Christmas campaign was not a rejection of Christmas, it was a celebration of it: a celebration of the fact that couples can enjoy an intimate, grown-up Christmas."

Lovehoney created its most ambitious TV ad campaign to date the following year, which ran for eight weeks from 17th November. It created two versions of the ad, one for between 9pm-11pm (no products, just box shots) and another for post-11pm. It consisted of actors reading out the words of Lovehoney customers over shots of products.

"Consumers are responding well to the ads," Lovehoney's Richard Longhurst said of the campaign. "They go straight to the website and can see the products featured on TV. We obviously get fewer viewers for the later ads, but they are proving to be much more effective in terms of conversions."

He also made a bold prediction: "As sex toys become increasingly part of the mainstream, you'll be seeing a lot more toys being left under the Christmas tree, particularly couples' toys. The days when we were a novelty purchase are long gone."

All this paid-for advertising was contributing to the continuous growth of the company, a Lovehoney spokesperson said, after the firm recorded the busiest day in its history in the run up to Valentine's Day 2016: "More people are hearing about us and when they come to the site they have a fantastic experience and come back," the spokesperson said. "We are taking sizeable chunks of market share from rivals, too."

And on Valentine's Day itself, the first part of yet another fly-on-the-wall series devoted to the company was broadcast. *The Joy of Sex Toys* was another collaboration with Oblong Films for the Lifetime channel and, like the preceding *Frisky Business*, it focused on 'character-driven storylines' which featured the firm's staff.

Richard Longhurst said: "TV has really worked for Lovehoney and helped us to market the brand globally. We have been lucky to work with a brilliant team at Oblong who are great at capturing the fun and excitement and occasional craziness of working for Britain's biggest online sex toy retailer."

More recently, US sex toy manufacturer Doc Johnson featured in the Amazon Prime docuseries, *This Giant Beast That is the Global Economy* in 2019. The show took viewers on a journey through some of the most complex issues of the global economy, using a comedic spin to help illustrate financial concepts, and Doc Johnson appeared in a lengthy segment of episode two. According to Doc Johnson COO Chad Braverman, the programme resulted in customers from all over the country calling and emailing in support of the company and its commitment to making products in the USA.

Finally, in 2022, several manufacturers reported increased sales after their products were featured in the raunchy Netflix interior design show, *How to Build a Sex Room*. Described by *The Guardian* as "*Changing Rooms* for sex people", the series followed designer Melanie Rose around the US as she helped people transform basements, bedrooms, and garden sheds into centres of pleasure.

Guardian reviewer Rebecca Nicholson wrote: "If, like me, you never suspected that a home makeover show could involve so many butt plugs, then welcome to the new wave of sex TV."

"Like the Fifty Shades of Grey collections, the toys were given names associated with memorable episodes, so the perfect add-on sale to the Respect Your Dick Vibrating Cock Ring was the Mind My Vagina Lubricant."

Are porn stars celebs? I feel the answer should be yes, if they are also known outside the world of porn. And on that basis, my introduction to celeb-endorsed – as opposed to porn star-endorsed – sex toys was the Jesse Jane collection from California Exotic Novelties (now known as just CalExotics). In early 2004 the US manufacturer sent our reviewer a box of samples which included Jesse's Futurotic Travel Pussy, Jesse's Vibro Pussy Sucker, Jesse's Magnetic Teaser, and Jesse's Climatic Climaxer.

Best known in the adult sector for starring in the *Pirates* series of pornographic movies by Digital Playground, Jesse qualifies as a celeb due to her mainstream appearances, which included a cameo in the *Starsky & Hutch* movie. She can also be seen brandishing a baseball bat on the cover of Drowning Pool's 2004 album *Desensitized*.

Jesse reportedly played an active role in the toys' development, attending creative meetings and choosing her favourite materials, colours, and scents for the products: "I cannot believe that the best masturbators I've ever used have my name on them," she enthused at the launch. As well as her name, the product boxes also sported a fetching image of her in her underwear.

Presumably the thinking behind such products was that men who watched her movies would quite like it if they could have sex with her too. But as they couldn't, a collection of items which they could have sex with, which had a connection to Jesse, would be seen to be the next best thing.

Jesse was far from being the first adult entertainment star to be available in take-home form. Early noughties adult shop shelves were packed with products endorsed by performers such as Tera Patrick, Jill Kelly, Jenna Haze, Monica Sweetheart, and Chasey Lain (who, it could be argued, qualifies as a celeb through being the subject of Bloodhound Gang's 2000 hit 'The Ballad of Chasey Lain') but the biggest name in town was Jenna Jameson.

Jenna was the world's best known porn star in the 1990s, which in itself surely makes her something of a celeb, but she also crossed over into the mainstream in a big way, like no one else before or since.

In 2001 alone, she was immortalised in cartoon form when she played herself in *Family Guy* (episode two of the third season, 'Brian Does Hollywood'), she appeared in the video for Eminem's 'Without Me' as one of the 'trailer park girls', and the Oxford Union debating society invited her to fly to the UK and argue against the proposition 'The House Believes that Porn is Harmful' (Jenna did, and her side won the debate).

Her 2004 autobiography spent six weeks on The New York Times Best Seller list and proof of her enduring popularity can be found on the shelves of today's adult stores, where products which carry her name and likeness can still be found.

It wasn't all about the girls: there was no shortage of larger-than-life-size (at least I hope they were) rubbery replicas of male porn stars' tools of the trade, available for fans to take home and appreciate. But did such endorsements drive sales?

In the early noughties *ETO* asked a number of manufacturers whether having a 'name' on the box helped sell a product, and the consensus was that it could, if the performer had a large enough profile. Back then, 'profile' generally meant DVD sales, whereas now it would be social media followers.

Interestingly, some of the manufacturers we spoke to believed having the name of a 'sexpert' on the box was even more beneficial than a porn star. "Products endorsed by experts in the sex field have a greater perceived value," said one contributor. Another said: "Whereas porn stars appeal to people's fantasies, sexperts tend to add credibility to toys and make them more socially acceptable."

California Exotic Novelties had recently collaborated with Sue Johanson for a range of toys, and a representative from the firm confirmed the accuracy of those comments, saying: "Our preliminary sales figures are huge."

Although not widely known this side of the Atlantic, the Canadian author, public speaker, sex educator, and media personality had a big following in the US where TV chat and phone-in show *Talk Sex with Sue Johanson* ran for six seasons in the noughties. I met her in Las Vegas at the launch of her toys and she was an absolute delight, talking me through her love balls, vibes, and butt plugs and even giving me a signed copy of her book, *Sex, Sex, and More Sex*. Ah, what a gilded life I once led...

The only UK porn star I can recall having a collection of branded sex toys was Ben Dover, who launched a small range of products to coincide with the cinema release of the mockumentary *Rabbit Fever* – more on that later – and it probably won't surprise you to learn that the first, to my knowledge, UK firm to use a sexpert to endorse its products was Lovehoney. The firm began working with Tracey Cox in 2005, and as it still has over 60 products on its website bearing the Tracey Cox branding, it seems safe to assume this was, and remains, a mutually beneficial relationship.

Things started to change in 2010, when male dance troupe The Chippendales endorsed the Diva massager. The Chippendales were neither porn stars nor sexperts, but they were well known for getting their kit off. And the fact that they were well known was probably reason enough for a company called Love Fun Play to attach their name to its 'sensual massager'.

Adding a famous name to a product has long been standard practice in mainstream marketing, and with good reason. Manufacturers hope a little of the celeb's stardust will attach itself to their product, and not only will it get more media coverage, but the celeb's endorsement should also increase the product's desirability. Ideally, the celeb will have something in common with the product but it's not absolutely necessary: think of former boxer George Foreman and what he's now best known for.

Celebrity Geordie duo Gary 'Gaz' Beadle and Charlotte Cosby did have something in common with the products they endorsed in 2014: the KNKY smart sex toys. For the uninitiated, Gaz and Charlotte were breakout stars of MTV's *Geordie Shore*, the UK version of the US constructed reality show *Jersey Shore*, which followed the daily lives of a bunch of young people living together. Described by one critic as "a gaudy kaleidoscope of six packs, shots, fights, simulated fellatio, and exposed breasts," *Geordie Shore* ran for over 20 seasons.

"Nobody has more sex than me," Gaz said in the press release for the KNKY launch, "so getting involved in designing a range of sex toys was an easy decision," while Charlotte added: "KNKY is a mint business venture for me – and one I am buzzing to be involved with."

KNKY was said to be the world's first his 'n' hers heated interactive vibrator range. The devices could be controlled by a smartphone app and Gaz and Charlotte, who had shares in the venture, fronted an Indiegogo crowdfunding campaign for it.

Unfortunately, my records do not reveal what happened next. You can still find KNKY on Facebook and Twitter, with images of Gaz and Charlotte, but the last activity on either platform was in 2015, so that probably does tell us what happened next.

Another reality TV star who launched her own range of sex toys in 2014 was Coco, the actress, dancer, glamour model, web personality, and wife of rapper Ice-T, who she starred with in the E! TV series *Ice Loves Coco*.

The Coco Licious collection was created in conjunction with California Exotic Novelties and the launch party in New York City was even covered by the UK's *Daily Mail*. Sadly, the report only made passing reference to the toys, focusing more on Coco's appearance: "The 35-year-old reality star wore a short sleeveless dress with a low-scoop front that displayed her bodacious bosom as she introduced her Coco Licious range," it read. "Coco, real name Nicole Natalie Austin, had her long blonde hair down and added a pop of colour with bright red lipstick at the event. Her lacy dress had a sexy cut-out back and was so short that it left her toned legs on show."

Good to know.

Those who have fame suddenly thrust upon them, perhaps through doing something unusual, tend to have a short shelf life in the public eye so the old saying 'strike while the iron is hot' is a mantra for firms seeking to cash in on their sudden popularity. Or indeed, notoriety. Pipedream recognised this in early 2015 when it created a range of toys in record time. The collection consisted of three toys – Library Girl Love Doll, Eager Beaver Stroker, and Cutie Booty Stroker – which were endorsed by Kendra Sunderland. She became famous in February 2015 after shooting a webcam scene in the Oregon State University library and footage of it went viral. 'Library Girl', as she became known, was quoted as saying she would love to have her own range of sex toys one day, which prompted Pipedream to offer her a reported six-figure sum to do just that.

Pipedream CEO Nick Orlandino said at the time: "Timing is everything and our ability to design, develop, and ship a brand-new collection in just over a week is what makes Pipedream so successful. We needed to come heavy while Kendra is still trending and we're confident that we nailed it with this release."

Kendra, who still enjoys a high profile in the world of adult entertainment and has almost 1m followers on Twitter, was not the only hot property at this time. Farrah Abraham first came to prominence in the TV series *16 and Pregnant* in 2009, and the subsequent spin-off, *Teen Mom*. Afterwards she released a music album and memoir, both of which were called *My Teenage Dream Ended*, and in 2013 she made a porn film called *Farrah Superstar: Backdoor Teen Mom*.

In 2015, Farrah appeared in Channel 5's *Celebrity Big Brother*, and retailers were urged to cash in on the resulting publicity by stocking the sex toys that carried her name. These included several vibrators, a stroker, an inflatable doll, and the Full-On Farrah Vibrating Pussy and Ass (for those who favour a missionary position) and Farrah's Backdoor Entry Vibrating

Pussy and Ass (for... you get the picture). Both P&A products were apparently moulded from Farrah's nether regions and featured hand painted lips.

You might be aware that US soft rockers Steely Dan took their name from a steam-powered strap-on which appeared in William S Burroughs' 1959 novel *Naked Lunch*, but the worlds of rock music and sex toys only really entered each other's orbits in 2008 when Dave Stewart – best known for being one half of the Eurythmics – offered his latest single, *Let's Do It Again*, free of charge to fans who bought a vibrator. The vibe had the song's lyrics printed on its shaft and the rather steep price tag of £1,000 could be partly justified by the inclusion of tiny diamonds around the tip.

Punk band The Vibrators put their name on a sex toy in 2011 – and if you think that sounds like a Lovehoney 'wheeze', you're right – when the Buzzin' Bullet was launched, complete with a 'gig proof' coffin-shaped metal case, and the following year California Exotic Novelties teamed up with Phil Varone to create the Sex, Toys, and Rock 'n' Roll collection. The former Skid Row and Saigon Kick drummer had his manhood cast to make the Dr Philgood dong, which was available in vibrating or non-vibrating versions and – like Phil – came with a removable Prince Albert piercing. There were eight other products in the collection, with the most interesting being Sex Stix, a pair of plastic vibrating drumsticks.

Celeb-endorsed sex toys reached a whole new level in 2015 with the launch of the Motörhead Official Pleasure Collection. It consisted of four vibrating bullets and torpedo-shaped vibes, decorated with the band's logo and branding and named after Motörhead songs, including 'Overkill' and 'Ace of Spades'.

"One of the songs on our debut album was called 'Vibrator' so we had to have our own one day, right?" Motörhead frontman Lemmy was quoted as saying in the press release for the launch.

The deal was brokered by Global Merchandising Services, who represented Motörhead for retail, tour and licensing, and its CEO, Barry Drinkwater, said: "Global is excited to be rockin' our clientele in such a fast-growing industry. We like nothing better than making the fans happy... and we're thrilled to be partnering with Lovehoney."

Doubts were expressed about this initiative by one or two industry veterans. Had Lovehoney gone too far this time? Did they really think sex shop customers would want to buy a vibe just because it had a rock band's name on it?

As it turned out, some of them did, but of far more significance was the global coverage this initiative picked up. It was an obvious quirky story for the mainstream media – 'Would you buy a Motörhead sex toy?' asked *The Guardian*'s Lost in Showbiz column – but it was also huge news in music circles, appealing to people who might never have even thought about sex toys before.

A Motörhead-themed window display dominated London's Oxford Street, courtesy of licensed retailer Harmony, and the range was distributed to a whole new market sector by European merchandise shop EMP, even though a piece in *Ultimate Classic Rock* suggested that Lemmy may not have actually been onboard with the process from the start: "They do a deal with our manager, then he tells us and it's too late to change it," he was quoted as saying. However, he added: "The sex toy thing was a surprise, but it seems to be working out."

It certainly did. So much so that the following year Lovehoney did it again, this time with Mötley Crüe. As before, each of the vibes in the collection was named after one of the band's songs and, also like before, the music media, including *NME, Classic Rock, Rolling Stone*, and *Team Rock* were delighted to spread the word.

The Independent ran a piece with the headline 'Mötley Crüe vibrators: how branded sex toys can sexually liberate fans', and Lovehoney's international sales manager Jim Primrose commented: "We've been blown away by the positive reaction from the world's media and our press team have been inundated with requests from top journalists and bloggers wanting to review the range."

Confirming that it could create a range of sex toys from the most unlikely source material, Lovehoney went on to launch a *Broad City* collection. The US TV show was described as 'an odd couple comedy about two best friends whose adventures always lead down unexpected and outlandish paths' – which included introducing pegging to a mainstream TV audience for what was believed to be the first time. Like the *Fifty Shades of Grey* collections, the toys were given names associated with memorable episodes, so the perfect add-on sale to the Respect Your Dick Vibrating Cock Ring was the Mind My Vagina Lubricant.

Some of those same industry veterans still puzzled by the Motörhead deal were even more perplexed by this branding exercise but, of course, it wasn't aimed at them. The stars of the show featured prominently in the launch publicity and the *Broad City* connection was an irresistible hook for mainstream media to hang their coverage of the toys on. So fashion and lifestyle sites such as *bustle.com, elle.com, self.com, nylon.com, dailydot.com, allure.com, femestella.com,* and many more, were delighted to inform their readers of the new arrivals.

It's also possible to get coverage just for designing a personalised gift for a celeb, as Doc Johnson proved in January 2016 when it created a unique present for actor Donnie Wahlberg to give to his wife, Jenny McCarthy. The one-off Donnie Dong was a conventional 8" silicone vibe up until its tip, which was a 3D recreation of the head of the former New Kids on the Block star. Jenny was presenting a radio show when Donnie handed over the gift, and she tweeted her delight to her followers, sharing a Doc Johnson discount code in the process.

If you're having trouble picturing what a dong with Donnie Wahlberg's head would look like, just search for #DonnieDong. And if you'd like a dong of your own with a celeb's face on, Marylin Manson's website is selling one that features his visage for $125.

Just a few words of praise from a celeb can be enough to introduce a brand to a whole new audience, as US manufacturer Sportsheets discovered on 28th August 2019, when traffic to its website broke all previous records, with hordes of consumers all buying the same thing. The traffic was coming from Kourtney Kardashian's lifestyle website, *Poosh*, which had featured the Sportsheets Peace Vibe as its #pooshpickoftheweek. *Poosh* posted the article to both its website and Instagram account, which had over three million followers at that time (it's got lots more now) and the Insta post clocked up 7,000 likes within a few minutes. The company reported even more interest in the vibe – and even more sales – after Kourtney Snapchatted about it.

But the biggest media splash of all was made by Lily Allen in October 2020. The British songstress was everywhere: advocating that women should openly talk about masturbation without guilt (*Daily Mail*), revealing that she didn't have her first orgasm until she was 29 (*Mamamia*), confessing that she resented men because she felt like "it was their responsibility to make me cum" (*Dazed*), and explaining that her sex life radically changed after she purchased her first sex toy (*Daily Mail* again).

These articles, and more in other outlets – including an interview the singer gave to BBC Radio 1's *Newsbeat* – provided the perfect platform for her to promote her collaboration with sex toy brand Womanizer.

Yes, I know, it is an unfortunate name, but I doubt it will be changed now. The German manufacturer introduced 'pleasure air technology' to sex toys in 2014, with the bold claim that it would deliver multiple orgasms without touching the clitoris. Rather astonishingly, this bold claim turned out to be a lot more than just hot air, and Lily became an advocate for the brand. Unofficially at first, writing about its products in her memoir, *My Thoughts Exactly*, and then joining the company as 'chief liberation officer' and heading up its #IMasturbate campaign, which was designed to raise awareness of sex positivity and female masturbation.

Lily also put her name and likeness on the box of a special edition of the Womanizer, called the Liberty, and she was certainly not shy about promoting the device during the media circus that surrounded her at the time.

Johanna Rief, head of sexual empowerment at Womanizer, said: "Lily is the embodiment of our brand: brave, honest, authentic, and approachable. We are happy and thankful that we share the same mission which is to wipe out the social stigma around sexuality and pleasure and make sure that future generations grow up in a more liberal and open-minded society."

The #IMasturbate campaign was conceived after a survey of 7,000 men and women from 14 countries conducted by the company revealed that while men masturbate 156 times per year, women only manage it 50 times.

"Sex toys are still seen as a taboo subject because they are related to masturbation and female pleasure," Lily was quoted as saying. "Female pleasure in itself is a taboo subject. The only way to make taboo subjects no longer taboo is to speak about them openly, frequently, and without shame or guilt."

Another A-lister was in the headlines the following month, for similar reasons, when Lora DiCarlo announced that model and actress Cara Delevingne was joining the firm as co-owner and creative advisor. According to the company, Cara would encourage people to embrace their sexuality with positivity and confidence, sharing their unified values of unapologetically celebrating sexual exploration and working to destigmatise sexuality.

Delevingne commented: "Lora DiCarlo's vision represents so much of what I stand for – women-led, femme-focused, and pleasure inclusive. I am so excited to step into this role as company co-owner and creative advisor, and contribute in a creative capacity with Lora and her team. Their award-winning products are redefining how people explore, experience, and take ownership of their pleasure."

Ah yes, award-winning. You may recall from the earlier chapter on PR that Lora DiCarlo was the firm that famously won a CES award, then didn't, then complained so loudly that it did again, so it was no stranger to media headlines. And this initiative certainly made plenty of those, not just in the lifestyle and fashion press but also in the business sections too.

A similar move was made by Dakota Johnson, who was perhaps best known for being the daughter of actors Don Johnson and Melanie Griffith, at least until she starred in the film version of *Fifty Shades of Grey*. In 2020, Johnson joined sex toy maker Maude as an investor and co-creative director.

Will this trend continue? Is someone working on a range of his 'n' hers' vibes with Posh and Becks branding? I can just picture the pair on the sofa of *This Morning* with Phil and Holly, holding up the Goldenballs collection for the camera. Such a move might be seen as controversial, but David has shown he's not afraid of a little hoo-ha. He did agree, after all, to be the face of the FIFA 2022 Qatar World Cup, an endorsement which raised eyebrows in many quarters.

Sadly I doubt it will happen, not least because neither David nor Victoria come cheap. I urge you not to Google how much the Beckhams earn from their existing endorsements, to spare you the existential crisis that will inevitably result.

While financial constraints might rule Posh and Becks out, it is still possible for sex toy brands to add a glamorous celeb's name to their box. In fact, Womanizer proved it is possible to have the face and name of the 20th century's best known sex symbol adorning its packaging in 2022 when it inked a deal with the estate of Marylin Monroe. The box of the resulting product – the Womanizer Classic 2 Marylin Monroe Special Edition – featured an iconic image of the Hollywood star and there was also an accompanying ad campaign called I Am Original.

Some might feel that using a dead celeb to endorse a sex toy is a step too far, and I might be one of them. The celeb obviously cannot personally consent to the arrangement, even if their estate can. *Cosmopolitan* was clearly okay with the licensing deal though, saying: "Sure, diamonds are a girl's best friend. But when Hollywood icon Marilyn Monroe first performed the hit song back in 1953, pleasure air technology had not been invented yet. Fast-forward to 2022 and we think you'll agree that, were Ms Monroe alive today, she would in fact declare that sex toys are her real gal pals, and clit-stimulation vibes would most definitely be her BFF."

Womanizer's head of sexual empowerment, Johanna Rief, said at the time of the launch: "We believe that Marilyn Monroe is a true original who has inspired and continues to inspire women across the globe. Our special edition is a tribute to her and is designed and positioned to empower all of the individuals around the world that identify as a woman to break through stereotypes, to be their true selves unapologetically and to define their own sexuality."

Given how large the pool of dead celebs is, it will be interesting to see if others follow where Womanizer have led. Is there a market for a rubbery replica of Errol Flynn's penis, for instance? I fear we may eventually find out.

"You deserve better than that if you're spending £50 on a pair of knickers. You deserve better than that no matter how much you're spending on knickers."

Although I started chapter one by saying that in the year 2000 'Ann Summers may not have been the only game in town, but it was the only game in most towns', I should add that the UK was also home to hundreds of 'traditional' sex shops, both licensed and unlicensed.

Remember PH Moriarty's portrayal of sex shop owner Hatchet Harry in Guy Richie's 1998 movie *Lock, Stock and Two Smoking Barrels*? The fearsome Harry, who notoriously beat a man to death with a rubber dildo, was unlike any sex shop owner I met during my time with *ETO*, thankfully, but sex shops in popular culture were usually unwelcoming places.

And with their blacked-out windows preventing passers-by from seeing in, so too were the real thing.

However, sex shops don't have opaque windows by choice. They are there because their local licencing authority insists upon them. 'All windows must be dressed or designed so as to prevent persons outside the licensed premises having a view of any part of the interior,' is a typical stipulation of a sex shop licence.

This inevitably made them look a bit seedy, and their customers were often depicted as being 'men in dirty raincoats'. Comedian Dom Joly capitalised on the fear of being spotted in one in his early noughties Channel 4 series, *Trigger Happy TV*. A man was surreptitiously filmed walking into a sex shop and while he was inside, Dom and his team set up outside around the entrance. Dom was dressed as a master of ceremonies, complete with mic and portable PA system, and accompanying him were a glamorous blonde holding a bottle of champagne, a brass band, and two men holding up an enormous sign that read 'Congratulations, 1,000,000th sex shop customer'. As the victim emerged from the store clutching his purchase, the brass band oompah-ed into life, Dom shouted "Congratulations!" and camera-wielding paparazzi pounced to capture the moment.

The location of licensed sex shops could often be a further impediment to attracting custom. Even the most enthusiastic estate agent would be forced to describe their positions, which were usually in the less salubrious parts of town, as "secondary", so it was a brave lone female who ventured through the doors of one for the first time in the 20th century.

One who did was Ky Hoyle. After graduating with a Fine Arts Degree from Brighton University and spending time in Japan teaching English, she returned to the UK and in 1991 visited a sex shop in London's Soho for the first time.

She later described the experience as "intimidating, alienating, and 100% directed at men", and thought the products on display were "graphic, ugly, and shockingly bad quality", concluding that the only women these sex shops catered for were the ones that needed a pump and had an always-open mouth.

So she did something about it. On 1st April 1992 she opened a shop of her own, called Sh!, in the Hoxton – before it became upmarket and trendy – area of London, with a budget of just £700. This might not sound like a promising start, but Hoyle was on a mission. The name of the new business was said to be "a playful comment on society's silencing of women's sexuality" for instance, and Hoyle's aim was to provide a boutique-like environment "where women could explore and discover their own, true, sexual selves rather than having it dictated to them".

If that sounds radical for the time, it was.

The Britain of 1992 was a very different country to today: an underwhelming Conservative party was in government; the England men's football team was underperforming on the world stage; and GDP was falling and interest rates rising because the country was in recession. Nothing like today at all, then.

It was certainly a less inclusive society though.

Sh! can justifiably claim to be the UK's most influential adult boutique. It really deserves a whole book to itself, and I'm sure it will get one at some point. Sh! had a bright pink interior and all-female staff, and to ensure customers felt safe in the store, men were only permitted in if they were accompanied by a woman. And even though it sold sex toys, its windows were not blacked out.

As you'd expect, this new store was soon enjoying plenty of coverage in UK newspapers and women's magazines, but this was just the start of the Sh! story. It was an early champion of the rabbit vibe, years before Charlotte and Miranda, and when it was unable to source dildos that met its expectations, it began making its own.

Predictably, the exposure the store was getting soon attracted the attentions of the local council, which concluded that because a 'significant' proportion of Sh!'s stock was made up of 'sexual articles' that the store should be licensed. This would result in a number of restrictions being placed on the store, including a ban on under 18s – so women would be unable to enter if they had a baby with them – and having to pay the not inconsiderable fee of £17,500 to Hackney council's licensing department every year.

When Sh! chose not to apply for a licence, the council took legal action. The case reached court in 1994 but thanks to the arguments made by defending Barrister Terry Munyard – who pointed out the absurdity of a feather duster being defined as a sex article – the case was thrown out and Sh! continued to trade without a licence.

Sh! produced its first catalogue in 1995, charging a small fee that was donated to the Breakthrough Breast Cancer charity, and it introduced its Gift Giving For Girls initiative in association with charities that support women's sexual health and wellbeing in December 2010. Customers could either make a donation themselves or on behalf of a friend, partner, or family member, and Sh! sent out a gift card stating that the person had donated a positive and practical gift that would make a real difference to a woman that Christmas.

"As well as a time for pleasure and treats, Christmas is also the time of year when we think of others less fortunate than ourselves," said Hoyle. "We know all about providing pleasure and we believe that a healthy, happy sexuality is crucial to a person's whole wellbeing. We wanted to help other women heal the damage done to them whether through sexual prejudice, ignorance, or violence. There are lots of charity gifts, but none that deal specifically with sexuality, so with the help of our charities, we created our own.

"As well as a practical means of helping women, this Gift Giving for Girls builds on our commitment to create important links between sexual health organisations, charities, and women's lobby groups and the so-called erotic industry. By working together we can help women everywhere heal, explore, and celebrate their sexuality, no matter what their circumstances."

As one of London's highest profile adult boutiques, Sh! had no shortage of celebrity customers over the years, but instead of trumpeting about them to the tabloids – like many an ambitious retailer would – it retained their custom by keeping their identities confidential. This added intrigue to the mix, and when Hoyle was invited to 10 Downing Street in 2002 for an AIDS Awareness event hosted by Cherie Blair, she refused to reveal the nature of the gift she brought for the hostess, leaving the watching media to draw their own conclusions.

Despite being behind many worthy initiatives, and the recipients of numerous awards over the years, Sh! closed its doors during the pandemic and they did not reopen. Instead, the retail business moved online entirely in 2021 and sexual wellness platform Shush Life was created.

Its aim was to inspire people to have imaginative sex with themselves and/or others, with courses designed to teach new techniques. "Shush Life is about giving people the permission to get into their bodies and out of their heads," Hoyle said at the launch. "Women, especially, have been constrained by lack of empowerment around their sex and sexuality. Shush Life is here to inspire people to have the imaginative sex and experience the pleasure they so very much deserve, especially at this time. The courses are based on the conversations about intimacy that we've had with the thousands of customers who have visited the shop or contacted us."

After the launch of Shush Life, Hoyle was interviewed for *The Mirror* newspaper and she said that putting the classes online had resulted in far more people being able to access them: "We now help around 500 people a week have orgasms," she was quoted as saying, giving the article its headline. This led to her being invited onto *This Morning* with Phil and Holly, and several other newspapers ran with the story.

The most recent Sh! initiative has been to partner with and help support Sex with Cancer, an online shop and public campaign that explores how people living with and beyond cancer can take agency over their own health and wellbeing.

Where Sh! led, others followed, and women-friendly stores blossomed in other towns and cities across the UK. These new 'boutiques' were rarely licensed so their windows could contain lingerie-wearing mannequins, and inside they showcased 'lotions and potions' in prominent positions while a curated selection of tasteful sex toys could be found in discreet locations in-store.

This new breed of retailer had more in common with Body Shop than a traditional sex shop and in 2003 The Me Company announced it would be taking the concept a stage further by opening stores selling 'female indulgence products' in high profile shopping centres. It opened its first branch – branded Meco – in The Glades, Bromley, in August 2003 and it intended having an additional five stores by the end of 2004.

The terms of Meco's lease stipulated that sex toys were to be of 'superior quality', not representative of either male or female body parts, not containing jelly or latex, and the packaging should have no nude images or sexually explicit words.

"We are delighted to be opening the Meco stores at such an exciting time in the development of the industry," MD Geoff Read said after the first branch opened its doors. "The opening went brilliantly, and the response was fantastic, bringing a smile to everyone's faces in the centre."

Unfortunately the smiles did not last and, in contrast to its loud arrival, it quietly disappeared without achieving its ambitious six-store rollout. Was Meco ahead of its time? Possibly, though its business model of offering a limited selection of upmarket products in prestigious shopping centres has not been replicated.

The retailers doing the real business in the early noughties were chains of licensed stores, such as Simply Pleasure, Pulse & Cocktails, Nice 'n' Naughty, Pillow Talk, Harmony, Soho Original, Clonezone, and Prowler – with the latter two targeting the gay community. These chains had grown, organically and through acquisition, to become formidable businesses and while they could never be confused with Meco, the owners knew it was in their interests to operate stores that were as welcoming as possible rather than just catering to the dwindling 'dirty raincoat' market.

The biggest chain of all was Private Shops, which opened its 100th store in October 2005. The business had been built on the sales of pornography, and its stores were a little old school, being a little rough around the edges in places.

But even Private became more female-friendly over the years. Boss Mike Wallace told me in 2014: "We wanted to get away from the shabby perception that some people have about licensed stores. Even now there are people who are too embarrassed to enter a traditional licensed shop, perhaps because they expect it to be male-focused, so we've tried to make our stores as welcoming as we can while still adhering to the licensing restrictions we are placed under by different councils."

Unfortunately these 'licensing restrictions' meant its modernising project became an agonisingly slow process. The Private management wanted to refresh its stores' appearance, interior displays, and stock profiles but approval was required from every individual council before any changes could be made. In some cases, I was told, the planning process just to change the exterior colour scheme took over a year and the associated costs ran to four figures.

A casual observer might suspect that councils disliked the chain. And they'd be right. One insider told me that dislike was far too mild a word for it: few councils wanted Private branches on their streets, particularly after the firm initiated legal proceedings against them following the Westminster case of 2012.

Lockdown was particularly hard on Private Shops, as its online operation was some way behind its rivals, and despite its best attempts at reinventing itself, its parent company fell into receivership in 2022.

I only ever had positive experiences when visiting sex shops but I commissioned a mystery shopper in 2004 to report on the UK's retailers for a regular feature in *ETO*, and it's fair to say the results were mixed, particularly among independent businesses. Like a spaghetti western viewer, our undercover reporter encountered the good, the bad, and the ugly but it was noticeable that standards generally appeared to rise every year.

One store I was looking forward to having a root around in was Hustler Hollywood. I first learned that the US chain of superstores was coming to the UK while visiting a wholesaler for a profile article in late 2003. After the CEO had finished showing me around his warehouse – an essential element of every wholesaler profile piece – we returned to his office where his assistant said he had to ring a certain person from 'Hush for Hollywood' (sic). He was confused by this – as was I – because the person who had left him that message was a senior buyer for a well-known high street retail chain.

The news was confirmed in March 2004, when it emerged that Hustler Hollywood was opening branches in Birmingham and London, with plans for more stores the following year. Unlike its American counterparts, the UK business would not stock hardcore movies, magazines, or 'extreme' sex toys, concentrating instead on lingerie, toiletries, 'soft' male and female toys, books, and clothing, negating the need to grapple with the UK's draconian licensing regulations. According to media reports, some £33m was going to be spent on the project, which was a joint venture between the US operation and a group of British investors.

The Birmingham store was opened by Hustler founder Larry Flynt in October 2004, to much media fanfare. The 6,000 square foot store, spread over two floors, was said to be the largest of its type in the UK. It certainly had the highest profile of any British erotic emporium, being situated in a prime location in Birmingham city centre, with Marks & Spencer and Boots as its neighbours.

The projected annual turnover of the store was £2.5m, which meant the good folk of Birmingham would have to buy a lot of £20 'It ain't gonna lick itself' T-shirts without the 'harder' – and generally more profitable – side of the industry portfolio being represented in-store.

Hustler-branded clothing in all its forms, plus bags, shoes, and hats, filled much of the space and when our mystery shopper visited, they noticed that the sex toys that were there were not showcased in a particularly customer-friendly way: "The boxed items were all priced on the bottom, making 'subtle' browsing impossible," our reporter said. "If you wanted to know the price, you had to show interest by picking it up."

Nevertheless, in April 2005 a second, more modest, branch of Hustler Hollywood opened in the heartland of the UK adult industry, Brewer Street, Soho. Hustler Hollywood UK chief executive Andrew Joseph told me: "As serious players in our industry, we had to have a presence there while we are waiting for the perfect store [in London] to come up. We have the investment ready for the right place in London and we are looking for sizeable premises."

In addition to opening a flagship location in the capital, there were plans to open branches in Glasgow, Leeds, Cardiff, and Newcastle in 2005, and Joseph was also talking to third parties regarding concessions: "We have been approached by every major department store concession asking us about our range," he told me. "We are now in the process of deciding who we wish to work with, because we do not want to overflood the market."

Sadly there was no danger of that. Both branches closed in November 2005, and the Hustler Hollywood UK website was replaced by a holding page. But Andrew Joseph told me this unhappy state of affairs was only temporary: "The stores are closed because we need to reposition ourselves within the marketplace," he said. "We've realised that we needed to change our product mix to get to the level we want to be at."

He added that he'd invested a further £5m in the business and sold 25% of the company to outside investors for an additional £5m, and this £10m investment would be used to roll out the next stage of the company's development: "We've got sites in Cardiff, Leeds, Newcastle, Glasgow, Manchester and Camden," he said, "and all six stores could be open for Valentine's Day 2006."

The Soho branch did open again in December, but only for a brief period, and in April 2006 the party was officially over when the US operation released a written statement saying it had chosen to terminate its licensing agreement with Hustler Hollywood UK.

Should the Hustler Hollywood concept be resurrected in the UK now, it would probably have more chance of success, as well-run 'superstores' like Pulse & Cocktails continue to thrive, despite the general downturn in physical retail sales.

Pulse & Cocktails operates 17 stores across the UK and although it tends to keep a low profile it does pop up in the media from time to time, usually when a reporter discovers that several former Little Chef roadside restaurants are now offering weary travellers stimulation rather than sustenance. In a June 2013 *Daily Mail* article, MD Graham Kidd told the tabloid: "Our sexy superstores are all about creating a fun, safe, couple-friendly environment. Recently, we have found a bit of niche by redeveloping redundant roadside diners… We have found our new roadside locations trade very well."

Although its stores are smaller in size than Pulse & Cocktails, the Simply Pleasure chain has a larger number of outlets, and individual branches frequently collected five-star reviews from our mystery shopper. In 2021 alone, four of its stores received top marks including Bournemouth ("A diverse and very rewarding shop to explore"), Exeter ("All you could want from a sex shop"), Mansfield ("A delightful location"), and Swansea ("Quirky products, well presented… exactly what adult retail needs to survive against Amazon").

Other chains worth mentioning include Clonezone and Nice 'n' Naughty and the UK is blessed with many excellent independent adult stores, including Harmony in London's Oxford Street, Luke & Jack in Glasgow, Saints & Sinners in Blackpool, Scandals in Birkenhead, Taboo in Brighton, and Vibez Adult Store in Aylesford.

Leading gay-focused stores include Fetch in London, Fetters in Warwick, Gear and Prowler, both in London, Q Store in Edinburgh, and Regulation in London. All of these stores can stand comparison with the best-in-class of any other retail sector, and they are all run by lovely people.

There are many others I could mention, but I tend to skip lists when reading so assuming you do too I'll just add one final one: Coco de Mer in London's Covent Garden.

An upmarket erotic boutique, rather than a sex shop, it was opened in 2001 by Sam Roddick, daughter of Body Shop founder Anita Roddick, and it offered discerning customers a selection of ethically sourced designer lingerie, sex toys, jewellery, and erotic art.

With its founder's background, Coco de Mer was always going to enjoy a high profile in the media, and a roster of celebrity customers kept it there over the years, but in December 2011 Roddick decided a decade of running the store was enough and she handed the keys over to Richard Longhurst and Neal Slateford.

This seemed a bit of an odd move for the Lovehoney founders. They'd previously told me they had no interest in traditional retail, and whatever income the shop brought in would be peanuts compared to their existing business, but – as always – they were looking at a much bigger picture. Richard told me in 2012: "The reason it came to us was basically it needed saving – it's a fantastic brand with massive recognition and high-end luxury cache but the reality was that the business was in a mess. So it was either going to be closed down or sold off."

"Even my mother had heard of it and she struggles to remember the name of *this* company," said Neal, before revealing the real appeal of the deal. "That kind of recognition would cost you, if you were starting from scratch, millions and millions of pounds. It's associated with sex, it's upmarket, and it's known around the world: there is so much upside to the brand that the actual nuts and bolts of sorting out the shop are fairly minor compared to its potential."

Richard told me what some of those nuts and bolts consisted of: "The first job was to rescue the website so people could actually buy things from it," he said. "The customer promise was all over the place, it was almost like 'We'll send your order when we get round to it'. You deserve better than that if you're spending £50 on a pair of knickers. You deserve better than that no matter how much you're spending on knickers."

As with some of Lovehoney's previous acquisitions, the name Coco de Mer opened new doors for the business – but it worked both ways, as Lovehoney was also able to take Coco de Mer in new directions, most notably with the launch of a branded range of upmarket toys in 2016. Coco de Mer MD Lucy Litwack described the collection as "luxurious and decadent", adding, "We are entering a new era of opulence with lovers of sensual joy sparing no expense in finding pleasure products of the highest luxury."

And no expense was spared creating imagery for the collection, which was shot by fashion and portrait photographer Rankin – whose previous subjects included Kate Moss, Madonna, David Bowie, and HM the Queen.

The Coco de Mer Pleasure Collection was said to be inspired by some of history's granddames of seduction and included the Nell Pleasure Seed Vibrator. The bumph said the product 'recalls the life of Charles II's long-time mistress, Nell Gwyn, who was regarded as a living embodiment of the spirit of Restoration England'. It added that Nell grew up in Covent Garden, just a stone's throw from Coco de Mer's store, and that the vibe was available in both silicone and limited-edition gold – the latter coming encased in 18 carat gold plate and presented in an artisanal wooden box with gold detailing.

Just the one, madam? That will be £10,000 please…

Although 'luxury' sex toys were nothing new, the marketing of this range was something we'd never seen before. The Rankin product shots captured the vibes ornately displayed in a series of elaborate glass domes and gilded cages, and Litwack enthused: "Everything about the range oozes decadence. Based around the idea of exploration and discovery, encountering the unexpected, and using Coco de Mer's famous heritage prints, the packaging features a seductive peephole, subtly teasing people with the erotic prints that lay behind."

Could Lovehoney have created such a range without Coco de Mer? Of course. But would it have had as much cachet and attracted as much attention around the world? Unlikely. With the acquisition seemingly having achieved its purpose, Lovehoney sold the store to Lucy Litwack in 2017.

Prior to joining Coco de Mer, Litwack had spent six years with Victoria's Secret in the US and held director positions at La Perla, New Zealand-based lingerie business Bendon, and she had also developed and launched David Beckham's Bodywear range globally through H&M, so the Coco de Mer store looked to be in safe hands.

"I had about half a second in which I realised an orgasm had happened before the second one started, and I turned back into that weirdly gurning sexual banshee again…"

If you've got an interest in a niche area, there's a strong chance there will be a specialist magazine serving it. As well as general interest publications and narrow-focus titles jostling for space in the competitive sectors such as fitness, gaming, and motoring, your local WH Smith either stocks, or will order for you, magazines devoted to everything from cabinetmaking to canal boats, and from papercrafting to permaculture solutions – that one was new to me, too – plus hundreds more. In fact, the WH Smith website will sell you a subscription to over 680 different magazines, but none of them will be devoted to sex toys.

There never has been such a magazine in the UK, despite the increasing popularity of the products over the last two decades. Some may find this omission all the more surprising considering even philatelic enthusiasts have a choice of two – *Stamp Magazine* and *Stamp Collector* – devoted to their hobby.

I can only assume that sex toys was thought to be a niche too far by publishers, and such a magazine would fail to attract enough readers or advertisers. It can't have been because they considered the subject too risqué, not when they've happily published titles such as *Forum*, *For Women*, *Desire*, *The Erotic Review*, *Foreplay*, and *Filament*. And it can't have been a fear of newsagents not supporting it, as most were quite happy to fill their top shelves with soft porn from the likes of *Penthouse* and *Playboy*.

We'll probably never find out if *Adult Toy World* or *Pleasure Products Review* would have flourished as anyone launching a new consumer magazine in 2023, in any sector, would be considered 'brave' when so many titles are seeing their circulations falling.

The closest the UK came to getting a sex toys magazine was probably *Scarlet*. Launched in 2004, it aimed to 'reflect the changing attitudes to women and their sexuality' and this editorial remit very much included sex toys.

So much so that its glitzy launch party, where guests rubbed shoulders with actor Daniel Schutzmann, former madam Cynthia Payne, and reality TV star Jodie Marsh, was sponsored by online retailer Sextoys.co.uk. "At last there is a magazine that is the perfect platform for our products," commented the firm's PR manager. "Other magazines have specific sections dedicated to sex but this is a whole magazine specifically aimed at sexually confident women, meaning there is no wastage for us."

Scarlet certainly looked the part, sharing the same production values as any other glossy women's magazine, and as an added bonus it was guaranteed to be 100% diet-free. "So many women feel bad about themselves after reading a magazine," explained editor Sarah Hedley. "With *Scarlet* we want women to finish the mag feeling sexier than they ever have before – and from readers' letters it looks like we're achieving our goal."

Despite its success – or maybe because of it – *Scarlet* was sold by Helix Media in 2008 to Blaze Publishing whose portfolio included *Classic Arms & Militaria*, *Clay Shooting*, *Gun Trade News*, and *Sporting Rifle*: no sex but plenty of pistols, you might say.

The magazine's erstwhile publisher and Helix MD Gavin Griffiths commented: "I had achieved all I wanted to with *Scarlet*. Everyone said it was impossible to get a women's sex magazine into the mainstream and *Scarlet* now sells in WH Smith, Tesco and Asda – you can't get more mainstream than that."

Scarlet was sold again the following year, this time to Interactive Publishing, whose CEO Justin Sanders said "the continued uncertainty within the economy" had given the firm the opportunity to acquire the title. 'Uncertainty' was a mild word for it: the UK was deep in recession in 2009, with long-established high street retail chains blinking out of existence on a weekly basis and the financial sector on the brink of collapse, and the following year *Scarlet* ceased publishing completely.

Sex toys still had a presence on the newsstands though, appearing regularly in female-focused magazines such as *Cosmopolitan*, *Elle*, *Glamour*, and *Marie Claire*, and *Good Housekeeping* did occasional roundups of the best toys on the market in its 'Tried & Tested' section.

You could even see the toys in action… well, you could if you bought the December 2013 issue of *Cosmopolitan*, which ran an innovative ad from retailer Adult Toys UK. It included a QR code which, when scanned by a smartphone, took the reader to a YouTube video featuring behavioural psychologist Jo Hemmings presenting her top ten sex toys for Christmas.

Jo was a familiar face to viewers of reality TV shows like *Big Brother* and the five-minute video showcased items such as the Official Fifty Shades of Grey Beginner's Bondage Kit, saucy board game Nookii, and vibes from Jimmyjane, Lelo, Swan, and Rocks-Off. And the number one choice? Why that would be Jo's own recently published book, *Sizzling Sex: Turning the Heat Up on Your Sex Life*, since you ask.

Although I wasn't a habitual reader of glossy women's magazines, I found out pretty quickly when a sex toy picked up favourable coverage – because the manufacturer's PR team would issue a gushing press release stating their delight that such a respected authority as [*insert magazine name here*] had been so impressed with their product. As well as blowing their own trumpet, these press releases also served to mobilise the trade into stocking up with that item, as mainstream coverage inevitably resulted in increased consumer demand for whatever had been featured.

As an aside, one of these stories provided me with the opportunity to write my own version of one of the publishing world's most famous headlines. US brand Jopen had reported a surge in sales after its Callie Vibrating Mini Wand starred in the October 2016 issue of *Cosmopolitan*. The Cosmo reviewer enthused, "If Apple made a vibe, this would be it. Its seven patterns go from low to whoa!" and Jopen stated that demand for the product had been so strong it had completely sold out.

I couldn't resist it. My *ETO* headline for the story read: 'Super Callie goes ballistic, surge is quite ferocious', a homage to the *Liverpool Echo* original from the 1970s (when Liverpool's Ian Callaghan had played particularly well against Queens Park Rangers: 'Super Cally goes ballistic, QPR atrocious').

The Sun had also run a similar headline on a match report in 1991, and I was feeling quite pleased with myself, especially when an influential tweeter with lots of followers said nice things about it. But not all of this person's followers agreed: one rather bluntly said I should be sacked for theft rather than praised.

Hearst Corporation, the publishers of *Cosmopolitan*, must have noticed the impact its 'Sex Toy of the Month' feature was generating because in 2018 it launched its own brand of products. Retailers were supplied with a free-standing display unit, with branding in that distinctive typeface, to house the seven toys (including rabbits, wands, a G-spot vibe, and a bullet), several lubes, massage oil, and toy cleaner.

Created by Romance Brands, I flippantly asked the firm's UK distributor if getting the *Cosmo* endorsement had just been a case of taking the editor out to lunch, and I was told the process was "as challenging as you would expect" and had taken two years from concept to launch.

Interestingly, there were limitations on where it could be sold. "Hearst are, understandably, fiercely protective of their brand and only want it to be associated with companies that have similar brand appeal and ethos to their own," my contact explained. "All companies who wish to sell the range online will need to complete an agreement that says they will not sell through any online marketplaces such as eBay and Amazon."

The display stand, and the whole range, seemed targeted at the mainstream, and the distributor expected sales to come from newcomers to the market – people who may have fancied trying a sex toy but hadn't yet done so: "*Cosmopolitan* has been talking to women in the mainstream for over 40 years and has built up brand trust and many loyal fans along the way," I was told. "Women from 16 to 60 know and respect the brand and will therefore feel empowered to try a *Cosmo* branded toy."

Elle magazine seemed even keener to get its readers into sex toys, by quite literally giving them one in 2019. 35,000 US subscribers were given the option of receiving a Satisfyer Traveler with their copy of the April issue. Those who opted in received their issue, which featured Taylor Swift on the cover, plus a box etched with the words 'The next sexual revolution' which contained the Satisfyer product. "This unique experience is a novel concept for the receivers of the subscription box and for the givers, *Elle* and Satisfyer," said a Satisfyer spokesperson in a statement. "The first feedback confirmed that this operation was incredibly successful."

But however welcoming consumer magazines have been over the last two decades, they have only ever been able to give sex toys a limited amount of space in each issue. And, even if a magazine does decide to include a specific toy, production schedules can mean it will be several months before it appears in print.

If only there was a way of getting writers to generate comprehensive reviews of products, and to turn them around in days... And wouldn't it be great if they could also photograph the product themselves and then tell the world about their experiences – at no cost to the manufacturer other than that of the toy being reviewed?

Long before being an influencer became a viable career option, blogging platforms such as WordPress and Blogger allowed people with a penchant for prose to monetise both their sex lives and their opinions.

They tended to be passionate about their work and would give far more attention to a product, while often revealing remarkably candid information about their sexual preferences, than any professional print journalist would. Some would photograph every aspect of the item being reviewed, and as broadband speeds increased they added audio and eventually video.

Whether they were recounting their saucy sexual adventures or forensically examining the features of the Ass-Gasm Pro P-Spot Milker (yes, this product exists) they could be rewarded for their labours through selling advertising on their site, becoming an affiliate of a retailer or manufacturer, or by directing their traffic to whoever was paying the most or was most in tune with their personal ethos.

The emergence of bloggers was wonderful for manufacturers, as even the most niche item could benefit from exposure for no more than the cost of posting out a sample. The market leaders were quick to realise their importance, and how they could be mobilised to make the most impact for a major launch. When Lovehoney launched its Sqweel in 2009, it sent a sample out to 100 top bloggers with an NDA (non-disclosure agreement) and an embargo date. When that date arrived, they all posted their reviews at once, creating such a stir that the event was covered on mainstream business and technology sites.

The arrival of social media platforms gave bloggers even more influence. Not only could they use Facebook, Twitter, Instagram etc to flag up content on their sites and grow their following, but 'sponsored posts' also gave them an additional revenue stream: and one blogger – Cara Sutra – was so high profile she even released her own branded product, the Beginner's Bondage Kit.

While having 100 bloggers writing about the same product at the same time will undoubtedly contribute to its success, sometimes just one is enough. Girl on the Net's 2014 post about the Doxy Massager, the debut product from a new company from Cornwall, was a key driver in its subsequent popularity: "I get frequent requests from companies to review sex toys, and previously I've always said no, because I figured I'd struggle to say anything other than 'this feels pretty nice on my cunt'," she wrote.

"I don't have any such problems with the Doxy, because holy clit-battering hell, this thing is amazing… It didn't just make me come. It did this weird and incredible holding-pattern thing, where I came just to the edge of orgasm then thrashed about on that plateau until I could barely see, speak, or do anything other than push back against it as hard as possible, grit my teeth and beg for the first waves to hit…

"After a few minutes in this happy-scary-horny Utopia, the waves eventually did hit, kept right on hitting, then dragged me off the ravaged coastline of my keening arousal and swept me out for more. I had about half a second in which I realised an orgasm had happened before the second one started, and I turned back into that weirdly gurning sexual banshee again…"

The full report, complete with a few sound samples, can still be found on Girl on the Net's site. And if you're looking for other sex toy bloggers you might want to check out *Kinkly.com's* annual Top 100 Sex Blogging Superheroes list.

Some bloggers became so successful they turned their part-time pursuit into a full-time career, and it's not unknown for their reviewing services to be in such demand that they now demand a fee in addition to a product sample – which seems absolutely fair.

Bloggers tend to be, by definition, opinionated. This can obviously be great for manufacturers whose toys win their favour but they are also able – and willing – to hold manufacturers to account for releasing shoddy product, using inappropriate language or imagery on their packaging, or even just choosing the wrong spokesperson (I'm thinking particularly of Lelo's decision to appoint Charlie Sheen as brand ambassador for its Hex condom in 2016). While being on the receiving end of their wrath has proven uncomfortable for manufacturers, bloggers' criticism has undoubtedly helped to raise industry standards and highlight missteps for others to avoid.

Although social media gave bloggers an even louder voice, it also allowed brands to communicate directly with their customers, and millions of other potential customers, for the first time. Now they could put up a Facebook post or send a tweet, as often as they liked and for practically no charge, that would be seen instantly, so it was no surprise that adult brands rushed to embrace these new platforms.

But social media required content. The odd gratuitous plug was acceptable, but brands needed to do more than just auto-post variations on an 'Aren't we fabulous?' theme to retain and grow followers. For example, Ann Summers took to the streets in 2012 in an ice cream van for its 'I Scream' tour. In conjunction with sex toy maker Screaming O, Ann Summers gave out free ice creams in London, Birmingham, Manchester, Liverpool, and Newcastle to members of the public who allowed their 'o' face to be photographed.

Initiatives like this certainly paid off. Katie Byrne, the firm's PR & social media manager, said at the time that Ann Summers' percentage growth for followers and engagement was up 1,203% compared to the previous year, elevating it into Digital Strategy Consulting's Top 20 of social media power brands for the first time. She attributed this success to not bombarding followers with posts, using unique content for each platform, rarely linking to products or promotions, and sticking to on-brand topical and reactive messaging.

And over ten years later, they still sound like good principals.

The four main social media platforms today are Facebook, Twitter, Instagram, and TikTok (though there could be something else as well, by the time you read this) and between them they would appear to offer everything a sex toy brand needs to communicate with its customers. But there are caveats.

Starting with Facebook, individuals are required to simply write some text, add an image, and click on 'post' to tell the world their news. With businesses, it's different: they are encouraged to 'boost' their post for a nominal fee so more people will see it. As of the time of writing, an investment of £8 will mean between 170 and 500 people will see my post each day for seven days. Upping the budget to £500 will result in an estimated reach of between 7k and 20k per day.

Sounds good? Unfortunately for sex toy brands, the Facebook of 2023 is a bit of a prude, and the boosting page carries this message: "Ads must not promote the sale or use of adult products or services. Ads promoting sexual and reproductive health products or services, such as contraception and family planning, must be targeted to people aged 18 and older, and must not focus on sexual pleasure."

Not focus on sexual pleasure? Welcome back to the 1950s.

And break the rules at your peril. Even an otherwise anodyne post about a new phallic dong, for instance, can result in the poster being kicked off the platform for a short period if the accompanying image is too 'realistic'. And repeat offenders' risk having their account deleted altogether, losing all their followers.

There are workarounds but most sex toy brands' Facebook pages adhere to the rules and, as a result, can look rather dull. There are no 'o' faces being pulled on the Ann Summers page, for instance, just wall to wall lingerie, tastefully shot – with an occasional non-phallic toy popping its cheeky head up.

Twitter is more lenient, and brands with big followings include Ann Summers (100k), Lovehoney (65k), Doc Johnson (47k), Lelo (38k), We-Vibe (35k), Bondara (30k), Fun Factory (24k), and CalExotics (20k). A method of directly and instantly communicating with so many customers would seem like science fiction to businesses of the last century, and a post with widespread appeal can travel around the world in seconds and be seen by millions if it gets retweeted or highlighted by the right people.

Barrack Obama, Justin Bieber, Katy Perry, Rihanna, Elon Musk, and Cristiano Ronaldo all have over 100m followers each, although I don't think any of them have ever mentioned a sex toy in their tweets.

If someone does mention a brand's product, the brand will get to hear about it if they're tagged in the text or the tweeter has used a recognised hashtag. There is a downside to being highly visible though, and posts that travel outside of an account's echo chamber of enthusiastic supporters can attract unwanted attention from trolls.

Photo and video sharing platform Instagram is said to be good for not only showcasing a product or company but also driving traffic to sites which can then be converted into sales. But like Facebook, which acquired the firm in 2012, it can be prudish when it comes to sex-related content, and offenders will be susceptible to bans, unable to boost their posts or buy ads, and having their account closed. It pays to follow the rules, because even if a member of the public doesn't report transgressions, you can bet that a competitor will. I'm told that video sharing platform TikTok can be even more stringent in this regard.

But following each platform's rules while also bringing something new to the party can prove lucrative. Vush is a relatively recent entrant to the market, having been founded in 2019 in Melbourne, Australia, and its website's About Us section, pointedly states: 'We're working to change the conversation around sexual wellness for you, but to do that, we had to create products worth talking about.'

It continues: 'Our range is a combination of everything we've always wanted sex toys and intimate care to be: inclusive, empowering, high quality, fun to use, and aesthetically beautiful. Gone are the days of hiding things at the bottom of sock drawers and back of bathroom cabinets; there's no shame in the self-love game, especially when the self-love products look this good.'

It wasn't just Vush who thought so: the firm's Majesty 2 wand was featured in rapper Cardi B's music video, *Up*. At the time of writing Vush has more than 600,000 Instagram followers. I strongly suspect the two previous sentences are not unrelated to each other.

Interacting on social media platforms has become part of many people's daily routine, and so too is listening to podcasts. Whether commuting, exercising, or just relaxing, a good podcast can whisk the listener away to a whole new world, background noise permitting, and according to *Statista.com* there were 19 million of us podders in 2021 and this is forecast to rise to 28 million by 2026.

The UK's first sex toys podcast that I was aware of was launched in 2007 by *Sexshop365.co.uk* and each monthly episode showcased new products, answered listeners' questions, and featured key industry players. While a number of other brands also have their own podcasts, others have found success by linking up with some of the sector's leading names, and one of the most prominent is Dr Emily Morse.

Although the focus of *Sex with Emily* is on sex and relationships, Emily has worked with a variety of sex toy brands during her podcasting career and her reach is now enormous: her podcast is said to be the number one in iTunes' sexuality category and there have been over 1,300 episodes – so completists will have quite some catching up to do.

Over the last two decades, consumer magazines, blogs, social media, and podcasts have all played a vital role in delivering the message that sex toys can be rather enjoyable, and as new platforms emerge in the coming years, I'm sure that sex toy manufacturers and retailers – which tend to be run by pretty smart people – will be among the first to embrace them.

"We are always on the lookout for new opportunities to help our customers live well for less and they've told us that sexual wellbeing is an area they would like to see more choice in."

Niche product categories usually developed along similar lines in the 20th century. First there were enthusiastic hobbyists devoted to the category, and then specialist stores would spring up to service their needs. Some became quite successful, opening additional branches around their region, but once the product had sufficient mainstream appeal the national chains would appear and say: "That's a nice little sector – we'll have it."

This happened in everything from DIY to video games. When the market was developing, word of mouth among enthusiasts would ensure a new specialist store had no need to advertise. At least until one of the national chains moved into their patch or their local supermarket cherry-picked the sector's bestsellers and retailed them for less than the specialist could buy them for.

The 21st century's leading retailers no longer operate on the high street but from cavernous sheds on retail parks or the internet. And they haven't just driven out most of the independent specialists, they've also seen off many national chains too, with inevitable results for the power dynamic between supplier and retailer. The biggest retailers can pretty much dictate what price they will pay for a product, stipulate when they will settle the invoice, and deflect back any risk of it not selling to the supplier.

This unhappy situation was often engineered by those very same suppliers. It was typical for emerging sectors to be fragmented: there might have been thousands of small retailers jostling for attention and hundreds of suppliers hustling for their business, and it was bloody hard work for a supplier to reach all those retailers.

The usual routes were taking stands at trade exhibitions, advertising in B2B magazines devoted to the sector, and employing telesales staff and 'road warrior' reps to build relationships. It was an expensive process. And that's before we take into consideration any retailers who would go out of business without settling their bills.

So if the nationals showed interest in the sector, suppliers tended to go out of their way to smooth their passage into the market. In addition to selecting the bestselling lines for them, suppliers might have arranged in-store merchandising and training of staff, contributed to their marketing budget, and even curated a selection of products exclusively for them, which the supplier's other retail accounts could not access.

Furthermore, this new account would be charged less for the products, be given a lot longer to pay the invoice, and would be protected from any risk by SOR (sale or return – if it doesn't sell, the supplier would take back the stock).

When details of these initiatives were leaked, which they frequently were, the supplier's other customers would be less than pleased to learn how their years of loyalty was being repaid.

"We helped build this market, and now you're handing it to our competitors!"

"No," the supplier would argue. "We're broadening the market. The people who shop in this new place won't be the same people who shop in your store, and they only have a very small range. When customers are ready to move on, they will come to you, with your extensive stockholding and your personal service."

"That's if I'm still trading."

It's understandable that individual shopkeepers will feel betrayed when their suppliers court non-specialists, but sectors tend to need the support of retail's biggest names if they are to go mainstream.

But can sex toys, by definition, ever go truly mainstream?

You're not going to see an Extra Girthy Realistic 10" Dildo, with thick, veiny shaft, pronounced head and textured balls, on the shelves of your local supermarket or pharmacy anytime soon.

Those retailers are not targeting customers who want life-size replicas of erect penises, they're targeting customers who want an 'intimate massager' that looks indistinguishable from any other personal care product, and they've been dipping their toes into the water since high street pharmacy chain Boots took out full page ads in the *Mail On Sunday* newspaper, and its female-focused colour supplement *You,* for the Vielle clitoral massager in 2004.

The ads featured a close-up of a happy couple in bed alongside the tagline, 'The simple way to improve your sex life'. You had to look closely to see a shot of the boxed product though, which sat discreetly in a corner of the page. The product was also being stocked in Tesco though I don't recall seeing any ads to that effect.

That same year, Tabooboo opened a concession in Selfridges and inked a deal to supply ten branches of Debenhams with a small selection of sex toys. Tabooboo claimed to be the creators of the world's first sex toy vending machine, and it was targeting bars, clubs, gyms, hotels, hair salons, and other retail outlets with the concept.

Addressing the Debenhams deal, and rumours that Boots and Superdrug would be stocking the recently introduced Durex Play range of products, a spokesperson for pressure group Family and Youth Concern, commented: "Family stores need to consider very carefully the messages they may be sending out to young people. If they go down this line, they will cheapen their image. The sexualisation of the high street is clearly an unwelcome trend."

And, rather surprisingly, it was considered to be in some areas of the adult trade too. In a forum-style article in *ETO*, concerns were expressed about whether a high street store, frequented by mothers with children and young teenagers, was an appropriate setting for sex toys.

Several contributors saw the upside though, pointing out that the media coverage was giving the sex toy sector legitimacy, that the participation of national chains would help to raise standards across the board, and that these stores could introduce sex toys to a new category of buyer, all of which would benefit the whole market.

But one person – who candidly told me he had been trying, unsuccessfully, to supply the chains – explained that moving into sex toys would not necessarily be the licence to print money these new retailers expected it to be: "A lot of big companies don't research the market properly before they dip their toe in the water," he said. "They do deals with people who aren't best placed to give them the best opportunity in the market. There have been a couple of occasions where we've seen sex toys appearing in high street locations very quietly and then going away again, because the toys they've taken have been the same old things which have been produced forever."

The rumours about Boots and Superdrug wanting to climb on the bandwagon were true but, perhaps as a result of the media backlash, Christmas came and went without them entering the market. It wasn't until July 2005 that Superdrug began trialling the Durex Play range in a selection of its Scottish stores. Sales must have been encouraging as the range was rolled out throughout Superdrug's UK stores in November and Durex Play Vibrations became the first sex toy to be advertised on a terrestrial television channel in the UK.

November 2005 also saw another household name move into the market: Amazon. And although it was the US .com site, rather than the UK's .co.uk, as a harbinger of what might be coming it was scarier than a *Stranger Things* trailer. Located under Health & Personal Care, then the sub-group Sex & Sensuality, Amazon's adult offering was split into four sections: Contraceptives, Romantic Delights, Sexual Enhancers, and Vibrators.

During my trawl of the site there were 4,740 lines listed under Contraceptives, with a 36 pack of Trojan condoms being offered for $9.99 against an SRP of $14.99.

Romantic Delights had 2,348 items and an edible bra was $3.71 as opposed to its list price of $11.13.

Arriving at the 6,747-strong Sexual Enhancers section, the prices really started tumbling: a Glitter Glam Slim Line Lady Finger Massager was reduced from $19.99 to just .69c.

Browsing through 7,970 vibrators I saw the Next Generation Rabbit Pearl Deluxe vibe for $19.99 ($49.99 list), Natural Contours 1320 Ultime for $13.99 ($34.95 list), and a Dual Dancing Silver Bullet Egg for $4.99 ($29.99 list).

Visitors could search for products by keyword, price, or brand, and most of the big names of the day were represented on the site. I fully expected US conservatives to register their displeasure at Amazon's new section, but I didn't hear any howls of outrage. I can only assume they never found out about it as it was a bit of a faff to find.

It was another year before sex toys appeared on the UK Amazon site, and even then they snuck in by the back door. A supplier of 18-certificate DVDs collaborated with a sex toy manufacturer to create two gift boxes – called Secret Suburban Sex Parties and Total Exposure – for the forthcoming Christmas shopping frenzy ("Ooh soft porn *and* a sex toy, how festive!"). In addition to the DVD and the toy, each gift box came with a sample of flavoured lube and a condom.

At the time, this was the only way UK consumers could buy sex toys from Amazon, but that exclusivity lasted little more than a month, and in December 2006 the trickle became a flood when the online retailer added hundreds of additional products to its portfolio.

In common with its US counterpart, finding the sex toys was also a bit of a faff on the UK site. Typing 'sex toy' in the search box brought up nothing of significance, but scrolling down to the bottom of the page revealed the following text: 'These search results have been filtered to remove adult products – click here to include these items in your results'.

This was obviously big news in the industry, and it was the front-page lead on the issue of *ETO* that accompanied me to a Las Vegas trade show in January 2007. I was chatting to a US manufacturer who clocked the Amazon story on the cover and looked at me incredulously.

They asked if it was true.

I assured them it was.

They replied that such a thing would never happen in America.

I explained that it already had, and our pre-smartphone conversation ended with them scurrying off to find a laptop to see for themselves. No wonder there had been no outcry from

US conservatives, when even people within the sex toy sector itself were unaware of Amazon's initiative.

It wasn't until September 2008 that a recognised name in consumer electronics decided to join the party by launching its own sex toy. But Philips didn't call its creation a sex toy. The Intimate Massager – a non-penetrative pebble-shaped device – was the lead line in the Dutch electronics giant's new Relationship Care category. There were three variations on offer: Warm Intimate Massager, Intimate Massager with Candlelights, and Intimate Dual Massagers, with retail prices ranging from £79.99 to £89.99.

The UK was the only European territory the Intimate Massagers were being launched in, after Philips said its research suggested the sector here was worth around €70m per year.

It was confident there would be a warm welcome for the device, citing a study it had conducted that indicated 35% of adults would consider using an intimate accessory with their partner if it was designed for couples rather than meant for individual use, and they would be more likely to try such products if they could buy them through 'more accessible' retail channels. So the trilogy of Intimate Massagers was available through Boots, Selfridges, and Amazon.

Sheila Struyck, head of market-driven innovation and category leader for relationship care within Philips' Consumer Lifestyle sector – who must have had quite the business card – commented: "This is an attractive market opportunity that Philips is in a unique position to pursue. We have the expertise in health and wellbeing, a strong track record in product design, a deep knowledge of consumer marketing, as well as a brand shown to lend credibility and appeal to this product category by addressing our target market in an accessible way."

I'm not sure Philips did demonstrate much knowledge of consumer marketing, nor an ability to address its target market in an accessible way, as I saw no evidence of any advertising, marketing, or promotion for these products – and believe me, I was *really* looking.

The launch did get a few mentions in the media, but it merited far more coverage than it got. A major consumer electronics manufacturer moving into sex toys should have been huge news, especially at that time – heck, it still would be now – so perhaps the Philips UK marketing department lacked enthusiasm for the product.

The next time I became aware of the Intimate Massager was 2010, when Philips announced it would be rolling out distribution into mainland Europe. This suggested it had been at least partly successful in the UK. Then again, it had been rebranded as the Sensual Massager, so maybe not. Either way, that was the last I heard of it.

More interesting than the device itself, which was pretty generic and similar to other 'massagers' from other manufacturers, was the annual value Philips attributed to the sex toys sector in its launch announcement (€70m, to save you going back).

That seemed quite conservative to me, especially as Ann Summers alone reportedly had a turnover in excess of £100m at this time. Obviously not everything Ann Summers sold was a sex toy, otherwise its stores would need to be licensed – let's not go there again – but there were literally hundreds of other stores up and down the country, and probably thousands of websites, dealing in sex toys at this time.

A more realistic figure was arrived at by market analysts Hewson Group, which published a report called *Women, Sex, and Shopping* in December 2008. Hewson Group concluded that the market at that time was worth around £400m, but it estimated that it could reach up to £1.1bn in five years, if it responded to what women wanted.

Hewson's research revealed that the sort of packaging and design that women wanted 'exists on a fairly exclusive basis, as does the nature of store design and store availability' as women wanted to purchase erotic goods in the same way they bought perfume.

Eponymous CEO Nick Hewson believed that Philips would be just the first big brand to enter the market, and he wrote in *ETO*: "This is a dynamic market with the potential for the fastest growth of all the retail sectors."

Hewson Group continued to research the sector, and in October 2011 it revealed the results of a huge study it had conducted among customers of female-owned adult boutiques, along with women its researchers encountered at locations such as cafes, bars, and railway stations.

There was a clear 3:1 preference for buying adult goods in a high street retail environment as opposed to online (the preference was actually 95% among customers of Sh! – and although only 44% overall said that buying erotic goods was an enjoyable experience, this almost doubled to 85% for Sh! customers).

Respondents were asked a number of questions about their ideal retail environment including where they would prefer to buy luxury sex toys. Given the option of a hotel, a cruise ship, a spa, a jeweller, or a hairdressing salon, 37% opted for a hotel. In response to another question only 6% said they would buy erotic goods from a supermarket.

Hewson concluded that the strong support for high street shopping refuted the idea that buying sex toys was 'embarrassing' and something women would rather do behind the anonymous cover of the internet. Indeed, the response to a later question suggested that over

60% of women found the idea of buying a sex toy arousing in itself, and this increased to 96% among those who completed their surveys in female-owned adult boutiques.

When I spoke to Nick Hewson, I asked him if he was surprised that no one had conducted any serious research into this market before his *Women, Sex, and Shopping* report of three years previously.

He replied that he was surprised then and was even more surprised now, adding: "The female consumer is very powerful in the world's leading economies, influencing around 80% of buying. Sexual goods for women have only been around, in practical terms, for a very short time but already we can see that they have become a significant factor in women's sex lives. The overlaps into massive sectors such as lingerie, beauty, fragrance, and luxury goods are very clear, and women see the connections. There are a lot of retailers and analysts who are slow off the mark in understanding the full implications of this."

The cost of the first *Women, Sex, and Shopping* report was a not inconsiderable £480, so it was interesting to learn who had been putting their hands in their pocket to catch sight of it: "Our main clients are from what you might describe as mainstream," Hewson said. "Retailers and retail analysts, lingerie brands, investment banks, luxury goods... Interest is growing as more people realise that this is an area where women might spend a lot of money and cross-buy into other sectors."

Hewson now doubted his previous estimate of what the market could be worth (£1.1bn by 2013) could be achieved, as he considered much of UK adult retail 'dysfunctional': "A lot of the adult industry aesthetic is really very poor indeed," he said. "Look at the best mainstream shops for women, they are used to some pretty classy merchandising.

"Also, and this is very important, older women have the money and adult shops don't really gear themselves to that market. That's commercial lunacy. We would be very critical of Ann Summers in that regard. Lovehoney have proved it can be done very well online by understanding their market, adapting their look, and doing the technical process in an outstanding way.

"Retailers should think who they are targeting, where the money is, and what the customer experience should be like. Pleasure goods is one of the sectors with the opportunity to provide a much more immersive and enticing customer experience. Women should walk into a store and not want to leave. Moreover, they should want to go back. We already see very different purchasing patterns in boutiques that get close to this."

If specialist adult retail was indeed 'dysfunctional' – Hewson's words, not mine – compared to other sectors, but offered a massive opportunity, then why weren't the national chains rushing in to grab it?

Holland and Barratt, which describes itself as the UK's leading retailer of vitamins, minerals, and herbal supplements, tentatively did, adding Emotional Bliss products to its website in 2009. The devices, described as intimate massagers, could be heated during use and the fairly abstract designs were pictured with pebbles.

Hmm. Remind you of anything?

One of the reasons behind the national chains' reluctance to rush in had to be the fear of a media backlash, and this was ably demonstrated in February 2012 when Boots added a small selection of sex toys to 1,200 of its 2,500 stores. The three non-phallic vibes – the recently launched Durex Play Discover, Delight, and Dream – could be found on an in-store 'Sexual Wellbeing' display, with the tagline 'Help you and your partner have a more positive sexual relationship'. Customers could see the products out of their boxes and the features of each model were listed on shelf talker cards. Just like any other product.

The *Daily Mail* fumed: "The chemists' chain has prominently displayed a range of unpackaged sex aids close to healthcare products such as reading glasses, blood-pressure monitors, and pregnancy testing kits. Customers have to walk past the sex aids in order to shop for shampoo, deodorants, toothpaste and sandwiches."

It added that the sale of such goods was "a far cry from the herbal medicines made by Boots founder John Boot in Nottingham in 1849" – though I'm not sure why. That point could equally be made about those blood-pressure monitors and pregnancy testing kits the 'sex aids' were displayed close to.

After that high profile push in Boots, Superdrug went even further in March 2013, adding a selection of lines from Ann Summers to the wellbeing sections of 25 of its stores. The range included seven varieties of Rampant Rabbits, along with jiggle balls, vibrating bullets and eggs, plus chocolate body paint and edible lubricants.

This initiative attracted the attention of *The Sun*. The tabloid sent a reporter into a central London branch with her five-year-old daughter and the subsequent piece – headlined 'We send mum out shopping in sexed-up Superdrug' – focused on the appropriateness of rabbits, 'c**k rings' and jiggle balls being offered in a 'family-friendly' shopping environment.

The challenge of browsing with an inquisitive child was referred to several times in the half-page article (sub-head 'Mummy, what's a jiggle ball?') but the only real issue the reporter had with the products was how they were displayed rather than what they were, pointing out, not unreasonably, that adult products on shelving at a child's eye level was not particularly conducive to a relaxing retail experience.

Another national chain joined the party in 2016, but I can't really say it complied with Nick Hewson's vision of pleasure goods being sold in an immersive environment with an enticing customer experience. Poundland rolled out the UK's cheapest sex toy, a dull pink coloured bullet vibe, to its 800+ stores and the media gave the firm more coverage that week than it had in the previous year. Probably.

According to Wikipedia, Poundland was attracting seven million shoppers every week in 2016, so what could they expect from their £1 sex toy? Not much, according to industry expert Alix Fox, who was commissioned by *The Sun* to compare Poundland's offering with six other vibes from established industry brands.

Fox rated the Poundland bullet the worst of the group, saying: "Many of us are on tight budgets, so the sweet relief of a little pleasure for just a pound is a steal of a deal – but it had just one speed and was loud and rattled like an OAP's false teeth during a turbulent flight. Not quite the hot night in I had hoped for."

Sure, it could be argued that she should not have expected much for such a small outlay, but I wonder how many people purchased the Poundland bullet as their first sex toy and then gave up on the whole sector?

There was no fear of that happening when supermarket chain Sainsbury's added three sex toys from Rocks-Off to its range in 2018. The British brand had been known for the quality of its products since its 2003 launch. Three vibes, retailing at £8, £12, and £15 respectively, were rolled out to 500 of the firm's stores as a result – according to contemporary reports – of research conducted by Oxford Economics and the National Centre for Social Research on the retailer's behalf.

Its Living Well Index found that people's wellbeing had fallen in the last year, particularly in the 'relationships' and 'social connections' categories, and Paul Mills-Hicks, food commercial director at Sainsbury's, was quoted as saying: "We are always on the lookout for new opportunities to help our customers live well for less and they've told us that sexual wellbeing is an area they would like to see more choice in. Our Living Well Index clearly shows this is an important area for customers' overall wellbeing. By introducing a new range at affordable prices, we hope to give customers the option to buy quickly and conveniently in an environment they feel comfortable with."

"Sales of bananas and cucumbers will fall drastically," commented one comedian under the *Daily Mail* report of the initiative, while another said, "Aldi's version, the Bratwurst 6000, can be found in its random isles (sic) next to the petrol woodchippers and sledgehammers".

Although the editorial itself was not disapproving, some comments certainly were: "People who use sex toys won't get into heaven, unless used in the context of a healthy marriage" claimed one, while another said, "I'm absolutely appalled at the thought of a supermarket selling sex toys where families with their kids shop."

Also in 2018, Boots took on seven toys from So Divine and the following year it added a selection of Lovehoney products to its portfolio, as did other pharmacy chains over the next 12 months, including Lloyds Pharmacy and the Republic of Ireland-based McCauley Health and Beauty Pharmacy.

Boots extended its relationship with the firm the following year when it added Lovehoney's Advent calendars to its website. Like scented candle collectors and bath bomb bon viveurs, sex toy enthusiasts have been brightening up their Decembers with 24 days of sexy surprises since 2005 when Orion Wholesale introduced the concept. The Lovehoney calendars retailed at £75 and £229: hardly impulse buys, though online retailer MegaPleasure later went further, introducing a £999 offering that laughed in the face of recession.

Writing in the October 2020 issue of *ETO*, Lovehoney national account manager Sarah Poole explained how the whole industry benefited when retailers such as Boots stocked its products: "Sex toys entering the mainstream retail sector serves as a pivotal step towards the further normalisation of sexual wellness and can act as a great introduction for people into our category, when they may not have necessarily considered using these types of products before. A positive introduction to the category, via a mainstream retailer, often leads initially hesitant customers to consider introducing more advanced toys to their sex lives, further supporting our industry."

There is no retailer more mainstream than Tesco, Britain's biggest supermarket with 26.9% market share. The firm introduced six Lovehoney toys to more than 250 Tesco Extra stores in February 2022, and these weren't just non-phallic bullets of the type that everybody else was stocking, there were also two rabbit vibes – a first for a UK supermarket, I believe.

There will inevitably be some industry insiders who still disapprove of mainstream chains selling sex toys, but it cannot be denied that such outlets have been instrumental in making pleasure products more socially acceptable over the last two decades.

They provide a gentle introduction to the sector for newcomers, although staff may not be able to advise on which vibe might be the most suitable for a customer's needs or which lube is appropriate for a given situation. Which is why there will always be room for independent specialist retailers, with friendly knowledgeable staff who understand their customers and the products they sell.

A few years ago I was having a drink with a veteran industry retailer who owned several stores, and we got on to the subject of the difference between a poorly performing store and a good one.

He summed up the difference in two words: the staff.

"The whole male sex toy industry is in its infancy and we aim to mainstream male attitudes to utilising sex aids – we aim to have Tenga do for men what the rabbit did for women."

A basic torpedo-style vibrator of today isn't hugely different to its predecessors from the start of the millennium. And those liberated ladies of the 1960s, who appropriated the Hitachi Magic Wand massage device for purposes other than relaxing their sore shoulder muscles, would instantly recognise the potential of today's market-leading devices from Doxy and Le Wand.

Perhaps the biggest difference between the toys of 2000 and 2023 is the sheer number of options that are available. Consider the humble wand massager: in addition to the original mains-powered device, the buyer of today can specify a low-priced battery powered version, a more upmarket USB rechargeable version, and a mini travel size version, in a wealth of different colours and a choice of materials.

The consumer can also customise their wand by pimping up its massage head with an additional attachment, usually available separately. These include clitoral teasers, G-spot and P-spot stimulators, masturbation sleeves for men, and even rabbit-style designs.

And speaking of rabbits – in this context, think of a vibrating phallic shaft with a twin-eared clitoral stimulator branching off it – comparing a state-of-the-art model of today, such as a Lelo Ina Wave, with the old Rabbit Pearl enjoyed by Miranda and Charlotte, is like comparing a Tesla Model S Plaid with a 1959 Ford Anglia. They do basically the same thing, but one does it rather more stylishly.

Today's rabbits come in a multitude of styles, and in addition to choosing the power and pattern of the vibrations, the consumer can opt for rabbits with warming, rippling, and thrusting functions. The more upmarket ones can be controlled via apps, and the consumer can even create and save their own vibration patterns.

Also enduringly popular are bullet vibes, which get their name from their shape. Usually quite compact, so they can fit in a handbag, the innocuous-looking devices come in several sizes and many colours.

One of the best-known manufacturers of bullets is Rocks-Off. Its bullets have metallic finishes and tapered tips, so they really do resemble their namesakes, and the company has tried to make them collectable by introducing limited editions such as its multicolour Summer of Love collection in 2017. Launched to mark the 50th anniversary of the original 'summer of love', the three bullets were named Groovy Baby, California Dreamin', and Be My Bo-Ho.

Torpedo, wand, rabbit, or bullet, every powered sex toy did pretty much the same thing up until 2015 when a new kid on the block arrived with the boldest claim that had ever been made in this sector. This new kid alleged it could do what no other sex toy could: deliver multiple orgasms without touching the clitoris.

Rather undermining this incredible claim was the name of this new product: Womanizer. It's not generally considered a compliment, and while I loved the Britney Spears song from 2008 – who doesn't? – I really doubted a product with a name like that would appeal to women.

'Hang about, Dale!' you might be thinking. 'Didn't Shakespeare say that a rose by any other name would smell as sweet?'

Yes, he did, but would roses be in such demand in the run up to 14th February if we chose to give them a different name, such as, I don't know, gussets?

"Verily, my true love hath procured for me a dozen red gussets for the forthcoming feast of Saint Valentine."

"Ooh, aren't thou a lucky cow?"

I digress. Womanizer was said to trigger orgasm by its application of 'pleasure air technology', gently 'sucking' the clitoris, with additional stimulation coming from delicate pulsating pressure waves.

It was unlike anything else on the market, resembling a digital ear thermometer but sounding like a flatulent steam engine. An unlikely combination but, for most women, it seemed to deliver on its claim. There was no friction generated by the orgasm, so hey, why not have another while you're here?

Womanizer took off like a Tesla Model S Plaid (for the record, the Tesla can go from nought to 60mph in just over two seconds, while the 1959 Ford Anglia we compared it to earlier would take 26.9 seconds to reach that speed), largely through word of mouth, reviews, and social media chatter. But while its name didn't seem to hinder its success, its £130 retail price meant it was out of the reach of many potential customers.

Nature is said to abhor a vacuum and the sex toy industry feels the same about a unique product that is successful, so there were soon lower-cost alternatives from other manufacturers, most notably Satisfyer, plus Womanizer itself, and now there is an abundance of 'air' toys available, in all different shapes, sizes, and price points.

Another product that created a new category was the Ruby Glow grind-on vibe, designed by erotic author and artist Tabitha Rayne. There had been ride-on sex machines before, such as the Sybian, but those were substantial in both size and price. Tabitha imagined something discreet, inexpensive, which could be used hands-free while seated: an interactive accessory for readers – and writers – of erotic fiction to grind on.

"I wanted to write through an orgasm, rather than having to take a break," she explained. "I wanted to 'go with the flow'. I thought it would be as simple as going online and buying what I required. This was back in 2014 when most sex toys seemed to be phallic dildos and rabbits designed for penetration or hard bullet vibes for clitoral stimulation. Having never been a fan of these sort of toys and rarely even trying them, I was disappointed that people like me weren't really catered for. Like, surely there were other folks who liked to hump and grind their way to satisfaction? I didn't even like sex toys touching my bare skin. It made me feel a bit alienated, so I abandoned the search and got out some clay."

Tabitha ended up with a design featuring a hump at one end, a dip, then a smaller hump at the front with a small pebble-shaped protrusion.

"I had a very clear vision of what I wanted — something that hinted at penetration at the vaginal entrance but no more, with a dip for the pubic bone then something for the clitoris to grind against," she said. "And because I'm a bit of a prude, I needed to be able to keep my knickers on while using it."

The resulting sculpture ticked all Tabitha's boxes, and that would have been the end of it if she hadn't shown the device to a friend, who encouraged her to share her creation with the world. If that sounds like an easy option, it wasn't (you can read the full story of Tabitha's fascinating journey on her blog) but the resulting product was eventually brought to market by Rocks-Off in 2015.

Rocks-Off MD Sue Walsh commented: "Ruby Glow is unique in as much as it's a dual motored product to be used while you are seated – for instance while reading a steamy book, skyping, or emailing a lover, perhaps watching an erotic movie at home, or maybe when you're in a chat room to add to your pleasure experience. The product is designed so it can be used through clothing, so that's a bit of a bonus which could really spice things up if you were enjoying Ruby Glow in a public area."

Tabitha added: "Ruby Glow is also great as a traditional clitoral vibrator and can be used in any position as it has lots of lovely dips and curves to press and grind against, even when you're standing up."

Ruby Glow obviously struck a chord, because it was joined in the market by the Vibe Pad from Orion (which looked like a slightly melted version of Tabitha's design), the Lust by CalExotics, and several other us-too products. Tabitha has since gone on to create updated and even more versatile versions of her original design.

With the honourable exception of Balldo, which utilises the testicles for penetrative 'ballsex', male toys tend to come in two basic flavours: those that go up the bum or those the user inserts his penis into.

There's quite a range of the former, in vibrating and non-vibrating varieties, while the latter encompasses everything from simple silicone tubes with a hole in (often called strokers, sleeves, or just masturbators) for under a tenner, to the hands-free Suck-O-Mat, which does exactly what you think it does and won't leave you much change from £300.

And if you think that's steep, that's peanuts compared to what discerning buyers of sex dolls are prepared to spend.

At the lower end of the sector are the basic blow-up babes so beloved of stag and hen parties. They often sport a face resembling a cartoon character opening an unexpected tax demand but spend a bit more and you can expect to find features such as a '3D' face, 'real' hair, one or two pieces of lingerie, a warming rod to make the spasm chasm feel more lifelike, and removable orifices, 'to make cleaning up a breeze'.

Go further up the range and your doll is likely to be made from soft silicone and have a stainless-steel skeleton, allowing you to pose it in whatever position you like. And if you don't find a doll you're attracted to, there are several places where – for the price of a decent pre-owned Ford Focus – you can specify every aspect of your doll's appearance, including her height, build, breast size, and eye colour. Be warned though: basing it on your best friend's wife will inevitably lead to awkward questions, though it would make for an intriguing episode of *Inside No. 9*.

Anyone who has more imagination than money, and is looking for an absolutely-no-frills entry level device, might want to consider a Water Woman, which resembles a child's swimming aid and is designed to be filled with warm water, but spend a little more and you can treat yourself to a Tenga.

When the Japanese product first hit the UK in 2007, it was described as an onanism cup and its launch bumph stated: "Tenga is not a sex toy but a highly sophisticated and ingeniously designed device capable of achieving a deep throat masturbation sensation that feels so realistic many men find it hard to believe it is not a human mouth."

Given their intended purpose, these cups – there were five models on offer – were incredibly over-engineered, with air cushion mechanisms, flexible alternating folds, angled nubs, rippled tightening zones, grainy and silky ripples, valves, pressure cabins, and lubricant reservoirs.

But the most incredible aspect of the product was that it was designed to be used just once.

I put it to Gregg Elliott of Passive Pleasure, Tenga's exclusive UK distributor at that time, that this seemed ridiculously wasteful.

"How can it be a waste?" Elliot retorted. "It's not a waste, it's an experience. Think of a nice bottle of red wine. You pop the cork and drink the wine but you only drink it once, and you savour every last drop. If you liked the wine you will buy it again. Tenga is the same. You pop the lid, savour every minute of the experience, and we know you will like it and be back for more."

But with Tenga single-use cups retailing at a tenner each, didn't this make male masturbation, for the first time in history, something of an extravagance?

"It's not expensive if it's viewed as an occasional treat or experience," Elliot replied. "We see Tenga as very much a treat, and if you use it occasionally you will really appreciate the experience. The whole male sex toy industry is in its infancy and we aim to mainstream male attitudes to utilising sex aids – we aim to have Tenga do for men what the rabbit did for women."

Reusable Tenga models were soon introduced, and the company celebrated shipping an astonishing 100 million units in December 2021. But it's not the best-known male sex toy: that honour belongs to Fleshlight.

Its name comes from its signature product, which resembles a torch, or flashlight – ah now the name makes sense – and has a removable cap that hides an opening for the user to put his penis into. The clever thing about a Fleshlight, certainly as far as men who live with other people are concerned, is that its exterior appearance is so innocuous it can be kept with tools and not attract a second glance.

Fleshlight pioneered this sector, bringing its first product to market in 1997. It went on to become a global market leader and it now sells a vast array of different models, all built on the same basic form: Fleshlight Signature Girls are based on individual female porn stars, with Fleshjack Boys being their male equivalents, and there are also hi-tech models and add-ons that resemble video gaming accessories. The Quickshot Turbo model even shares its name with a joystick popular with home computer owners of the 1980s.

The male sex toy sector got considerably more interesting in 2010 when upmarket German brand Fun Factory launched the Cobra Libre. Its design was said to have been inspired by the AC Cobra, a classic British sports car of the 1960s, and unlike other masturbation devices, Cobra Libre did not envelop the whole penis.

Just the head was placed in the cockpit (it wasn't called that, but it should have been) where two motors bounced vibration off each other. This resulted in an experience similar to a blowjob, and because the user was not required to move the device – he could either lie back hands-free, hold it in position, or relax while someone else held it – sessions could last a lot longer than the user might be accustomed to. In another first, it could even be used without an erection, allowing people with medical conditions which might prevent them masturbating conventionally to also enjoy a little me-time.

2013 saw the debut of British brand Hot Octopuss, with a new product called Pulse. Although very different in appearance to Cobra Libre, Pulse also relied on the penis resting within it, rather than the device being moved up and down. The savvy marketing team coined the term 'guybrator' for Pulse, which the pun-loving media absolutely lapped up.

The other type of male toys – the ones that go up the bum – are mostly either butt plugs or prostate stimulators. Plugs have evolved significantly in recent years and as well as vibrating they can also now thrust, pulsate, shake, and even inflate. Just be sure that any model you buy has a flared base – you don't want to provide the A&E staff with an amusing anecdote for their dinner parties.

As for vibrating prostate stimulators, the top of the market is served by feature-packed designs such as Lelo's Loki Wave, which retails at around £199, while those on a budget can get a basic no-brand from Amazon for under a tenner. Non-vibrating plugs and prostate stimulators obviously cost less.

As bums are universal, there is no real reason why anal toys should be considered a 'men only' zone, but that's the way they were often marketed, and you could have any colour you liked as long as it was black. Or fire engine red, for those who wanted to make a statement. That changed in 2016 when B-Vibe arrived.

Headed up by industry veteran Alicia Sinclair, B-Vibe brought contemporary branding and marketing to the sector with its first product, the vibrantly coloured Rimming Plug, and it now offers a wide range of anal products which have universal appeal, and they can be specified in vivid colours such as rose, teal, and mint.

As pleasurable as sex toys undoubtedly are, they tended to be seen as substitutes for people without a partner up until 2008 when a Canadian couple single-handedly invented a new category.

The We-Vibe was – and still is – a small flexible C-shaped device that is worn by the woman during sex. Each ridged end has a motor, one positioned to stimulate the woman's G-spot and the other to work on her clitoris. These two motors also provide 'harmonic pulsations' along the device, stimulating the shaft of the man's penis. Some early reviewers said that it also made the man feel bigger and the woman tighter, which is obviously a bonus. It could also be used on its own by a woman, and its snug fit meant it could even be worn while walking as there were no wires or straps.

It was conceived by Bruce and Melody Murison during a long car journey from New York to their home in Ontario in 2000. Bruce wondered if a product existed for couples to use while having sex, and he spent much of the next few weeks searching the web for one, coming up empty handed.

Both Bruce and Melody were employed by Canadian telecom firm Nortel – in the research and development area of the electronics department and semiconductor analysis, respectively – but when the dotcom bubble burst, the Murisons were among the thousands who lost their jobs, though their sizable severance package gave them the luxury of being able to choose their next career move.

Instead of returning to the tech industry, the siren cry of the sex toy that didn't exist pulled them in a different direction: "We thought the world needed a vibrator that fits between two people, and if you build it, they will come..." Bruce told me in 2008, simultaneously demonstrating his knowledge of Kevin Costner films and double-entendres.

Bruce had form in this area: his previous inventions had benefited the food service industry, lawn care, and Canada's only ice-breaking oil tanker, and he had extensive knowledge of mechanical engineering. He started with the motor configuration and settled on 3,000 rpm for the low-speed setting and 5,000 rpm for the high speed. This was arrived at after research among women volunteers revealed that a significant percentage of them found speeds above 5,000 rpm to be uncomfortable, and over half said that speeds as high as 9,000 rpm were just numbing. As there were no off-the-shelf motors that offered the power Bruce wanted with the diminutive size his new device demanded, he spent two years designing his own.

The first prototype was finished in 2002 but it was a further five years before Bruce was happy with what he'd created. And during all those years of her husband refining the design, Melody never once said to him, "Oh for goodness sake Bruce, it'll do!"

I know this because I asked her.

"I had faith in the invention," Melody said.

Which was just as well, as during We-Vibe's eight-year gestation period the Murisons were required to mortgage their house to finance its development.

After taking it to a US trade show, enquiries came in from all over the world and viewers of *Talk Sex with Sue Johanson* voted We-Vibe their Toy of the Year. The device went on to star at consumer and trade shows in Germany and London and has since sold millions of units worldwide. Word of mouth was a key factor in its success, according to Melody, who told me: "The best salesperson is a woman who has one."

One of the biggest changes I witnessed during my two decades in the industry concerned women. In the early noughties, when wholesalers often sold pornography as well as sex toys, most of the firms I encountered were run by men. There were exceptions, most notably Susan Colvin, the founder and CEO of US giant CalExotics, but generally at trade shows I was meeting people like me: middle-aged blokes.

As the noughties progressed, porn plummeted in importance as a product, due to it being freely available on the internet, and the focus of most wholesalers turned to sex toys. It had to, if they wanted to stay in business. But, to differentiate themselves from their competitors, they could no longer rely on generic imports from China and buying from the same American big brands as everyone else.

This competitive environment resulted in new sex toy brands receiving a very warm welcome, particularly if they were upmarket and offered a higher margin than their more mundane rivals.

And it turned out – who could have possibly guessed? – that the best people to design, package, and market intimate products aimed at women were other women. Trade shows grew in size to accommodate these new brands, many of which were run by smart successful women. Some were sex toy enthusiasts who thought they could create something better than the status quo, while others were savvy business professionals who spotted an opportunity to grab a slice of a growing worldwide market. And I'm sure some were both.

These new women-run brands were loved by the media, with some of the most successful being Biird, Bijoux Indiscrets, Crave, Dame Products, Le Wand (sister company to B-Vibe), Lora DiCarlo, Maude, MysteryVibe, Rianne S, and Unbound.

Not only did these firms create aspirational products, their marketing could stand comparison with luxury goods in other sectors, and their founders – being media savvy and exceedingly quotable – gave good copy to journalists

What was it Nick Hewson said earlier?

Ah yes: "Retailers should think who they are targeting, where the money is, and what the customer experience should be like. Pleasure goods is one of the sectors with the opportunity to provide a much more immersive and enticing customer experience."

Even if the retailers weren't listening, it seemed that someone was...

"Anyone expecting to masturbate the weight away would have to put in quite a bit of effort, as three ten-minute sessions a week would result in the loss of just 90 calories. Equivalent to a small bag of Quavers."

With sex toys being used in such intimate areas, one might assume the legislation surrounding their manufacture would be among the most stringent on the market. Unfortunately that is not the case.

At the start of the 21st century, a some sex toys were made from a soft jelly-like material, and few of us gave the subject much consideration. We really should have though. Poorer examples would degrade over time, leaving once proud and erect sculptures resembling the faces of the Nazis at the end of *Raiders of the Lost Ark*.

The issue was highlighted by the Netherlands division of environmental campaign group Greenpeace in October 2006, when it commissioned research organisation TNO to test eight different sex toys for phthalates. Usually added to plastics to enhance their flexibility and durability, there are both health and environmental concerns about their use, and TNO discovered that seven of the eight toys tested contained phthalates in concentrations varying from 24% to 51% percent.

"It is unbelievable that such toxic substances can be used in adult toys," Greenpeace spokesperson Bart van Opzeeland said. "We have tested many products in the last few years but never have we encountered such high concentrations."

The use of phthalates is a complicated business and the European Union's REACH (Registration, Evaluation, Authorisation, and Restriction of Chemicals) regulation is said to be the most complex in its history, encompassing 849 pages and taking seven years to pass, but progress has been made in recent years and now even modestly priced sex toys are often marked 'phthalate-free' on the box.

There is also an ISO standard for sex toys, but this wasn't introduced until 2021 when *ISO 3533 – Sex toys: Design and safety requirements for products in direct contact with genitalia, the anus, or both* was proposed by SIS (the Swedish Institute for Standards), in collaboration with 75 experts from 19 different countries.

ISO 3533's purpose was to increase consumer safety around pleasure products, after SIS noted the high number of surgical procedures carried out on patients admitted to hospital with objects stuck up their bum. "Sex toys are…a billion-dollar industry but until now there has been no international standard specific for this type of product," the SIS said at the launch of the initiative. "Without the guidance of clear standards with requirements specific for these products it is difficult for manufacturers, retailers, and consumers to know when a product is safe, and when it goes wrong it creates difficult cases for healthcare to handle... We now hope that manufacturers and other interested parties adopt this standard, making it a useful tool for quality and safety all around the world."

ISO 3533 covers the general requirements for risk management, design, materials, and user information, and goes into considerable detail. Design, for instance, includes sections on products intended for anal use, mechanical hazards, vibration, electrical safety, surface temperatures, and sharp edges and protruding parts, while materials cover safety, biocompatibility, and cleaning and maintenance.

Even if they haven't formally adopted ISO 3533, I would imagine the vast majority of today's manufacturers would already be following – or even exceeding – the guidelines, as I saw nothing in the document that could be considered unreasonable.

A large percentage of today's sex toys are made from either ABS plastic or silicone, which are both excellent choices, being non-porous, but those who might want their intimate products to be made from more natural materials have several options.

The creative shapes and eye-catching colours that can result from using glass gives such toys huge visual appeal. In addition to their aesthetic qualities, they also feel good in the hand, with their substantial weight combining with their smooth surface to give a reassuring feel of quality. Glass toys are also robust, easy to clean, and can be warmed or cooled before use.

In the early noughties, consumers could expect to pay around £100 for a glass toy but they now start at under £20: incredible value for something that could last a lifetime. They also make excellent ornaments in child-free homes, lighting up the room when catching the sun.

Glass toys have always been 'acoustic', relying on the user to do all the work, but they had their 'Dylan at Newport Folk Festival' moment in 2016 when Jopen launched its Opal massager. Jopen is the upmarket arm of CalExotics – as Lexus is to Toyota in the automotive sector – and the top half of Opal's shaft was made from curved glass while the bottom was made from silicone. The silicone section housed the multispeed motor and Opal even had a rabbit-style clit-stim.

Pipedream brought vibration to its glass Icicles collection in 2020 by creating a circular silicone base as an add-on. This not only contained the vibrating motor, but it also acted as a holder for the glass toy, allowing users to enjoy it hands-free with the supplied remote control.

Offering many of the same benefits as glass, stainless-steel is another material customers can specify their sex toy to be made from. US firm Njoy has been creating imaginatively designed shapes from this material since 2005, and in recent years it has been a popular choice for other manufacturers too. Stainless-steel sex toys are surprisingly affordable, considering how chic they look and feel, but one of the most desirable sex toys I encountered was made by a small Welsh company.

Mi-Su – it means 'rippling brook' in Native American, and it almost means 'buzz me' in Welsh – merged art, jewellery, and fashion in its creations. It was formed by Paul Ruscoe and Rebecca Doyle in 2003 with the aim of occupying the very tip of the top end of the market. It made three different products – plugs, dildos, and rings – but it was the materials they were created from that set Mi-Su apart from its competitors. It worked in titanium, obsidian, rose quartz, silver, and gold.

And, in the spirit of those M&S food ads, this wasn't just titanium, one of the strongest metals on Earth, this was solid hypoallergenic surgical grade titanium, able to sustain its temperature when heated or cooled and retain its original condition and lustre longer than any other precious metal.

I visited Mi-Su at its Port Talbot HQ in 2006, where Paul and Rebecca showed me the titanium dildo. It was heavy, and it felt expensive. Paul explained that it took between six and seven days to complete a single piece. The cost of the material was also far from cheap, and some of it was lost in the cutting, so prices started at £1,400, rising to £3,000 for a diamond-encrusted model.

I must have looked shocked because Rebecca said in mitigation: "The price of titanium has gone through the roof lately," which was the only time I ever heard that sentence during my time in the industry.

A decade later and Mi-Su's prices were made to look middle of the road by Swedish manufacturer Lelo. Its Luxe collection started at £1,690 while the top of the range Inez would set customers back a hefty £10,000 for the 24-karat gold-plated edition, and a hardly less astonishing £4,990 for the same design in stainless-steel. If it was a cynical ploy to attract the attention of the media, it worked – as anyone who googles '£10k gold sex toy' will confirm.

The very first dildos were made from organic materials, and while I don't imagine there would be much of a market today for sex toys sculpted from bone or horn, creating wooden phalluses has been a noble pursuit for skilled craftsmen for millennia. The labour involved in their creation usually priced such devices out of the mass market, but they could be found at fetish fairs, consumer exhibitions such as Erotica, and boutiques like Coco de Mer.

Wooden sex toys were first commodified, to my knowledge, in 2009 when Don Wands introduced a collection called Treeze. Made from a wood/urethane hybrid material that was said to be phthalate-free, hypo-allergenic, non-porous, waterproof, non-coated and splinter-free, the dildos and plugs featured replaceable internal vibrator units.

Those who fancy a dildo made from crystal might want to take a look at Chakrubs, which creates products that 'bring a sense of sacredness to your playtime'. The firm's website states: 'These beautiful, hand-crafted tools are created with the intention of opening oneself up to the healing properties crystals provide. Crystals have perfect molecular structures that have positive effects on our electro-magnetic fields. When our energetic bodies are at ease, we are at ease, we are open to healing, to peace, to love, to all of life's pleasures.'

Many of the price tags have three figures but the products are undeniably beautiful.

Although US manufacturer Pipedream built its business with conventional materials it was not slow to experiment with alternatives. It was one of the first to offer complete collections of toys made from glass (Icicles), stainless-steel (Metal Worx), aluminium (Pure Aluminium) and, most intriguingly of all, pottery.

Called Ceramix Pleasure Pottery, I first encountered it at a US trade show in 2013 and I was struck by the vivid colours, organic shapes, and tactile finishes. The toys looked like props from an 18-rated version of *Alice in Wonderland*. Whilst metal and glass toys can be gently cooled and warmed, Ceramix went further. The unique properties of the ceramic material, in conjunction with the hollow shafts, meant users could explore the extremes of the temperature scale.

Pipedream representatives demonstrated this at the show by filling Ceramix samples with hot and chilled water before shocking visitors to its stand who complied with requests to "feel this". The result was the hottest, and probably coldest, sex toy interaction this reporter has ever experienced.

There were 12 Ceramix toys, six vibrating and six non-vibrating, and they felt quite special. Ceramic is an earthy material that us humans have been connecting with for thousands of years and infusing it with Yttrium ensured it was also incredibly robust: I witnessed a Pipedream representative demonstrating this by banging a sample repeatedly against a wall. Although the vibrating models could not be filled with water, as they did not have hollow shafts, they demonstrated the material's insulating properties by being virtually inaudible in operation.

Designer Kristian Broms told me: "We worked on Ceramix for close to two years before we released it. It was a challenge from start to finish. From getting shapes that work to finding the right glazes it was quite a trip. Along the way we encountered more production issues than I care to recount. For example, different clay bodies differ in the way in which they respond when fired in the kiln. Finding a clay composition with just the right amount of plasticity and malleability was very important in order to control the amount of shrinkage that occurs during the firing process. The calculations have to be very precise for the vibrator assembly, caps, and silicone plugs to fit just right inside the finished pieces."

Broms added that the journey from raw material to finished product also took far longer than with materials like silicone: "There are no injection machines in the world capable of spitting these out. The art of pottery is more than 25,000 years old and involves forming clay into shapes and heating them to high temperatures in a kiln. To create this line we had to go back to the beginning of time in order to move forward.

"While we have more refined raw materials and better kilns these days, the process of producing these is still very much the same as it always has been. There is a lot of labour, a lot of drying time, hand-painting, handling, more drying time, firing in kilns, and tons of quality control. And this is all before these items even reach the assembly lines."

I'm not sure if the Ceramix range is still available – it's no longer listed on Pipedream's website and when even Amazon is out of stock one fears the worst – which would be a shame as the material, and the way it was decorated, gave the collection a distinctive look in a crowded marketplace. Persian Palm, from Italy, was its only rival, though I do recall seeing a lady from Dorset create similar items in the documentary *Inside The Sex Toy Factory*, which was broadcast in 2019.

Bells and whistles apart, many sex toys are pretty similar in appearance. This can partly be explained by the phrase 'form follows function' – meaning an object's shape should be dictated by its intended purpose – which is an accepted principal of design. Plus, the bigger a business gets, the more risk averse it becomes, and today's multinational corporations want their products to appeal to as many people as possible, so they'll often go with something similar to what sold well before.

But there is always room in the market for toys which bring something new to the table. And, like the Murisons with We-Vibe and Tabitha Rayne with Ruby Glow, individuals with inspired ideas can be responsible for creating a whole new category of products, with a little help from their friends and/or third-party agencies able to provide expertise in areas the inventor lacks.

Irish graphic artist Trevor Murphy sketched out his idea for a new sex toy and submitted it to Lovehoney's 2006 Design A Sex Toy competition. The fact that I've singled him out suggests something came of it, and indeed it did. The competition offered the winner a £1,000 cash prize plus, if the design was put into production, the opportunity to earn royalties from sales.

It took until 2009 for Trevor's idea to come to market but, when it did, the Sqweel was a huge success, even attracting the attention of US TV host Jay Leno, who demonstrated it on his show. The matt black device was inconspicuous in appearance – resembling a portable CD player – until its cover was removed, when its purpose became instantly clear. Imagine a small rotating wheel where every spoke is a soft silicone tongue.

By 2019, Trevor had reportedly earned over £300k from his oral sex simulator and every now and then his story, and generous remuneration, gets featured in the tabloids, particularly when Lovehoney announces a new Design A Sex Toy contest. "I made so much money that I was able to emigrate and start a new career in television," he was quoted as saying. "The competition completely changed my life."

Another individual with a singular vision was Shed Simove, a multi-talented entrepreneur with a talent for punning stunts who morphs between being a stand-up comedian, motivational speaker, author, and designer of novelty gifts. His back catalogue includes launching a brand of sweets called Clitoris Allsorts, posing as a schoolboy for a Channel 4 documentary when he was 30, changing his name by deed poll to God, and publishing a book called *Fifty Shades of Grey* in 2012 – which consisted of fifty totally blank pages, each in a different shade of grey.

In 2013 he moved into sex toys when he created the Masturpieces range of silicone dildos. What separated them from the crowd was their unique 'character' designs, which included Rampant Rabbi, Cunt Dracula, and Buckingham Phallus. The latter was a fairly detailed sculpture of the late Queen Elizabeth II, complete with crown, and Shed allegedly sent a sample to Her Majesty along with a letter asking her to endorse it if she agreed with him that it could give pleasure to millions of Britons.

This was clearly never going to happen, and not just because each Masturpiece model was limited to 100 units.

Shed used the Buckingham Phallus dildo as a prop during his one-man show, 'Trouble', but a small number of audience members reportedly walked out in disgust. Dozens more were said to have cancelled tickets for the show, after seeing a publicity shot of Simove brandishing the dildo.

If that actually happened then it was worth it for the resulting publicity, and if it didn't… well it gave us lazy journalists something to write about on a slow news day.

The Rampant Rabbi also grabbed a few column inches, after Shed applied for a trademark for the name – which was contested by a certain high street chain that had more than a casual interest in a similarly-named product.

While We-Vibe, Ruby Glow, and Sqweel are examples of successful sex toys designed by individuals, I could probably fill an entire book with examples of failures. In fact, look out for my next title, *50 Shades of Dismay: Sex Toys that Failed to Satisfy*.

Hmm, that actually sounds like fun, so I might have to do it.

If you feel you have an idea for a successful sex toy, there are specialist agencies within the industry, such as Sated Design and Concept to Consumer Collective, which offer services such as product and packaging design, engineering, marketing, logistics, and fulfilment – everything, in fact, that an inventor would need to turn a rough sketch into a finished product suitable for Tesco's shelves. Except money.

A popular method of raising capital for new concepts is crowdfunding, and one of the most successful sex toy inventors to use platforms such as Indiegogo is Brian Sloan. In 2019 he broke the crowdfunding record for a male sex toy when his Autoblow AI received over $750k in funding. As its name sort of alludes to, his device was said to use artificial intelligence to replicate the sensation of a blowjob.

Brian first came to prominence in 2014 when he was seeking funding for his Autoblow 2 oral sex simulator. He enthused: "I see a future where men own high tech masturbation appliances that are a normal part of their daily lives. The Autoblow 2 is the first step in that direction, and a giant leap towards improving the realism of the male masturbation experience."

Also looking to take a giant leap on Indiegogo in 2014, but in a different direction, was Teddy Love Incorporated, which sought backers for its eponymous product. Can you picture a 50 cm tall traditional cuddly teddy bear made from polyester fur? That's what Teddy Love was, but with a vibrating nose and tongue and controls in the ears. Teddy Love didn't reach its crowdfunding target but it still came to market, and *The Mirror* described it as 'The bear that loves you back' in a 2015 news story.

Also seeking finance through crowdfunding platforms for their creations were start-ups iGino, MysteryVibe, Odile, and Nadgerz (for, respectively, a discreet vibe that resembled an iPhone, a bendable vibe with six motors, a butt plug dilator, and a device which utilises the testicles for penetrative 'ballsex') but campaigns for new products have also been launched by established companies.

One of the earliest to do so was Norwegian brand Laid, which set up a fundraiser for its Loop interactive Kegel exerciser in 2014. Laid co-founder Karianne Ellekrans said: "Loop's final design has been tested, reviewed, and is ready for mass-manufacturing – but we currently can only afford to make a modest amount of units. With every Indiegogo pledge, we can increase our production numbers, speed up the process, and – most importantly – make Loop one of the industry's only interactive Kegel fitness systems that women of all lifestyles can afford to buy and use every day."

US manufacturer Tantus chose Indiegogo in 2015 to crowdfund its Rumble vibe, and Lelo sister company PicoBong announced that its Indiegogo campaign for its Remoji remote control app had raised five times its crowdfunding goal in 2016.

More recently, in 2021 Womanizer used Indiegogo to promote its Premium Eco, which it described as the world's first eco-friendly and biodegradable pleasure air toy. The campaign's purpose wasn't to raise money to develop the product though, but to prove there was a demand for sustainable sex toys. The campaign's £25k proceeds were earmarked for One Tree Planted, a US charity dedicated to helping global reforestation efforts.

When products eventually reach the shelves, one of the key factors determining their success is not their features or benefits but what they're housed in. Packaging dates back to when the very first products were traded, when its purpose was to protect the contents while they were being transported, but the packaging of today has two other, just as important, functions: to inform and to sell.

I try not to generalise, but early noughties sex toy packaging was, on the whole, pretty poor. Many were supplied either in a garishly coloured cardboard box or in a clear plastic clamshell with a garishly coloured backing card.

Rather surprisingly, given their target market, they frequently featured images of semi-naked women, with hairstyles from previous decades, pouting suggestively. This may have been because manufacturers expected their products to be bought by men, for women. Or maybe that is giving them too much credit, and the designers simply used the first 'sexy' image they could find that was cheap to licence.

Add in barely legible fonts that had been 'artistically' dicked about with, and language which some might deem offensive, and it's understandable why some of the new wave of online retailers chose to photograph their products out of the box and some stores displayed sample units 'naked'.

An honourable exception to this was Big Teaze Toys, a US brand whose flagship product was I Rub My Duckie. Imagine a cuter version of a traditional bright yellow bath duck, with big eyes, a pronounced beak, and a vibration function. Big Teaze Toys founder Tony Levine had a background in the children's toy sector and his company's packaging was as polished as its products, being eye-catching and colourful yet remaining tasteful.

I would also like to doff my cap to UK company Double G, which was best known for its Nookii board game for adults. In 2006 it introduced NookiiToy experiences. These were cardboard tubes, tastefully adorned with pastel colours, fun illustrations, and upmarket fonts, which were opened by pulling a ribbon on the top end cap.

Not only was the packaging ahead of its time, so was the concept: each tube contained a themed collection of toys and accessories, along with suggestion cards for their use. The idea was to move sex toys on from being products for singletons to being a fun package for couples to explore together: a laudable aim that suffered only from being ten or so years too early for the market.

In the same year, OhMiBod was formed in the US, and it was immediately obvious that one of the founders had previously worked in Apple's marketing department. The chic packaging was as slick as an iPod's, which was no coincidence as the eponymous product was designed to be used in conjunction with Apple's device, translating music into vibration.

One of the biggest drivers behind the improvement of sex toy packaging was manufacturers releasing collections rather than standalone products. There were sound business reasons behind this: why sell a retailer one cock ring when you can sell him 24 different versions?

With an accompanying planogram, the manufacturer could also show the retailer the best way to display the range. Collections could also benefit the store too: uniform packaging looks more professional than a hotch-potch of individual items, in different sized and coloured boxes, and collections tended to come with point-of-sale materials (POS), such as header cards for slatwall systems, catalogues, sample units, and sometimes even free-standing display units (FSDU).

Sex toy packaging of today is often the equal of any other desirable item of consumer electronics and, like your Ring doorbell and Tesla car, your toys can now be controlled by your smartphone.

The first toy to be app-enabled was the rather clumsily named We-Vibe 4 Plus in 2014. Users could not only control the device, they could also create custom vibration patterns and share control of it with another person, anywhere in the world. We-Vibe CEO Anne Finlayson said: "We-Vibe has been about connecting couples and building intimacy since the company's inception. With We-Vibe 4 Plus, we are bringing couples together, even when they are apart."

The following year, the We-Connect app was updated with voice, chat, and video and other brands started to join the party. 2016 witnessed Lovely getting coverage in media outlets such as the *Daily Mail*, *The Sun*, *The Independent*, *Glamour*, *Stuff*, *Engadget*, and *The Huffington Post* for its debut crowdfunded product, a vibrating cock ring. Not only could Lovely be controlled by a phone, it contained sensors which enabled it to learn what couples enjoy in bed and suggest ways they could perform better next time. It could even tell users how many calories they burned.

I can't comment on how successful the device was because I didn't hear anything else about it, and sifting through Google results for 'Lovely sex toy' would take the rest of my life. If nothing else, it will be remembered in these parts for the headline topping *The Sun's* coverage: 'RAMPANT TRACK-IT: Sex toy called 'Lovely' will measure men's performance and tell them if they're RUBBISH in bed'.

Zalo already had toys on the market when it introduced its app in 2019, which borrowed one of Lovely's more noteworthy features. 'Sex toy manufacturer's app now tells women how many calories they burn from using their vibrator,' purred the *Daily Mail* headline, which sounded exciting. It turned out that anyone expecting to masturbate the weight away would have to put in quite a bit of effort, as three ten-minute sessions a week would result in the loss of just 90 calories. Equivalent to a small bag of Quavers.

There is no shortage of app-enabled sex toys available now, and the brands mentioned above have been joined by the likes of Kiiroo, Lovense, MysteryVibe, OhMiBod, Svakom, Satisfyer, and Vibease, but arriving at this point was not without problems, as We-Vibe discovered when a class action was brought against parent company Standard Innovation.

A class action, known as group litigation in the UK, refers to a number of people with the same complaint caused by the same product or action suing the defendant as a group, and We-Vibe was accused of using its We-Connect app to harvest information about how its customers used its products, including the temperature and intensity settings users chose, without their knowledge.

The suit was filed in the North District of Illinois Eastern Division District Court by two anonymous users in September 2016, and it alleged that Standard Innovation was in violation of the Federal Wire Tap Act, Intrusion Upon Seclusion, and Unjust Enrichment.

Shortly after the litigation began, the legal teams of both parties met to discuss a settlement and agreed to resolve the matter through private mediation with Judge Morton Denlow (Ret) of Chicago-based Judicial Arbitration and Mediation Services Inc (JAMS). Standard Innovation denied every allegation and maintained that it had strong, meritorious defences to the claims, and it was prepared to defend itself in court, but it took the view that the uncertainty and risks inherent in any litigation would be protracted, burdensome, and expensive. The plaintiffs acknowledged that Standard Innovation had raised factual and legal defences in the action, and that there was a risk that the class action could ultimately fail, so both parties agreed to a 'full and final' settlement.

Standard Innovation agreed to pay four million Canadian dollars (just under £2.5m) into an App Settlement Fund and a further one million Canadian dollars (a little over £600,000) into a Purchaser Settlement Fund in 2017. US consumers who bought a We-Vibe Bluetooth-enabled device before 26th September 2016 but did not use the app could submit a claim for up to $199 (£121), while those who bought a device and used the app to control it could submit a claim for up to $10,000 (£6,127) from the funds. The payments were to be made pro rata, so the actual amount users received depended on how many claims were made.

Not surprisingly, We-Vibe swiftly updated its systems and processes to ensure such a case could never happen again.

"The coverage that The Official Pleasure Collection has received from mainstream media is phenomenal. No pleasure industry brand has ever received this level of coverage."

The first sex toy I saw in a mainstream Hollywood movie was the torpedo-style vibe Steve Martin's character Gil found, while looking for a torch during a power cut in his sister's house, in director Ron Howard's 1989 comedy/drama *Parenthood*. The vibe's on-screen time was very brief and the children in the movie were told it was an 'electric ear cleaner'.

I didn't see another sex toy on the silver screen until Mike Myers' swinging sixties spy spoof, *Austin Powers: International Man of Mystery* in 1997. The 'Swedish-made Penis Enlarger Pump' was apparently made by Pipedream, but the only branding the device carried was a Swedish flag, and – like whoever made the 'electric ear cleaner' – Pipedream didn't merit a mention in the credits. I know, because I checked.

The pump had a more significant role than *Parenthood's* vibe, as the cryogenically frozen Powers was thawed out and reunited with his possessions. His embarrassed attempts to distance himself from the device ultimately proved futile after it emerged he'd written a book about it.

If you thought penis pumps were medical devices rather than sex toys, you're mostly right. Their original purpose was to treat erectile dysfunction (ED): a user would insert his penis into the transparent tube and then manually pump out the air, creating a vacuum that drew blood into the penis, producing an erection. It's been claimed that regular use can increase both length and girth. The devices can also be used for masturbating, so they qualify as sex toys.

I am using the same premise to justify my inclusion of dolls as sex toys. Even the most basic model – something like Bondara's Jodie Juggs Lifesize Inflatable Sex Doll – offers buyers the choice of three openings for £16.99. Scoff all you like but, according to the single online review, the product is most definitely fit for purpose: "Mouth hole far too small for the average man. Pussy and arse are perfect fun. Can't go wrong for the price."

Ignoring any cameos by dolls on the lower end of the pricing and quality spectrum, the first mainstream movie to feature a sex doll in a supporting role was 2007's *Lars and the Real Girl*. It starred Ryan Gosling and Emily Mortimer alongside an example of one of US manufacturer Abyss Creations' RealDolls. These are a world away from Jodie Juggs – they have skeletons, so they can be posed, and buyers can customise almost every aspect of their RealDoll's appearance. Gosling had nothing but praise for his RealDoll co-star: "She did have a real presence," he told a reporter at the film's premiere. "This whole movie rested on our relationship together. She had a very supportive energy."

The movie is quirky, comedic, and poignant and even though Lars does not have physical relations with the doll, such exposure can only have helped the manufacturer, even allowing for the fact that its prices – upwards of $6,000 – are hardly impulse buys.

One manufacturer who reported immediate increases in sales following exposure in movies was Liberator, whose sex furniture appeared in both *Meet The Fockers* in 2004 and *Burn After Reading* in 2008. In the former, Barbara Streisand used the firm's Wedge and Ramp products while teaching a sexuality class for senior citizens. In the latter, George Clooney's character was a bit of a lothario, enjoying flings with Frances McDormand and Tilda Swinton, and he took a purple Ramp with him to assignations.

He also constructed an automatic fucking machine for less than $100 with parts he bought from Home Depot, which would have been the first time some viewers had encountered such a device. Frankly I doubt he could have made it for $100 though: it looked to be a high-quality construction, with beautifully fluid movements on the thrusting dildo.

George, if you're reading this, I'll buy as many as you can make at $100 a pop.

One of the world's best-known sex toys, the rabbit vibrator, had a whole movie devoted to it in 2006. The *Rabbit Fever* mockumentary (not to be confused with a genuine documentary of the same name, which focused on the National Convention of the American Rabbit Breeders' Association) had a cinema release and picked up plenty of mainstream coverage at the time, though not all of it was favourable. And when I say not all of it, I mean hardly any of it.

Billed as a light-hearted romp about a group of women in danger of becoming addicted to their rabbit vibes, it featured appearances from the likes of Julian Rhind-Tutt, Lisa B, Tara Summers, Flora Montgomery, Stefanie Powers, Tom Conti, Germaine Greer, Sir Richard Branson, Ben Dover, Sienna Guillory, Tom Hollander, and Emily Mortimer.

Germaine Greer lost no time in rubbishing the film in her *Guardian* column. In a piece dated 25th September, just after the film opened, she began by stating: "It's not easy sitting through a film about ugly, unhygienic vibrators – especially when you're in it."

She went on to call the movie "a stinker" and said that she only appeared in it because the parents of the casting director were old friends of hers. She added that when she made her contribution, she did not even realise that the rabbit vibrator existed, and she thought the scenario was pure fantasy.

The Ugly Truth topped the UK box office on its opening weekend in 2009, though critics were less than kind to the romcom, which starred Katherine Heigl and Gerard Butler. It earns its place in this chapter thanks to a scene featuring Dr Laura Berman's Astrea 1 Vibrating Briefs from CalExotics. Imagine a normal skimpy pair of lacey knickers but with a hidden pocket. In that pocket sits a small vibrator which can be controlled up to 12 feet away by a wireless remote control. Heigl's character wears the undies on a night out, and you can imagine what hilarity ensues when the wireless remote control falls into another character's hands.

The incident was described as "One of the funniest film moments since the orgasm scene from *When Harry Met Sally*," but that was by CalExotics CEO Susan Colvin, who may not have been completely unbiased.

Vibrators featured heavily in a 2011 romcom called *Hysteria*, starring Hugh Dancy and Maggie Gyllenhaal. Set in 1880, it purported to chart the birth of the sex toy through the medical management of 'hysteria'. The movie was based on historian Rachel Maines' 1999 book *The Technology of Orgasm*, which claimed that it was once common for medical professionals to treat hysteria in women by manually massaging their genitals, though this has been disputed. Whatever the merits of the central premise, the movie received a generally warm welcome from critics.

British sex toy brand Rocks-Off made its big screen debut in March 2014 in *Almost Married*, a comedy about a soon-to-be spliced couple (Philip McGinley and Emily Atack) and the consequences of a stag night visit to a working girl with a large sex toy collection.

More recently, Pipedream's Ultimate Fantasy Kitty Doll featured in *Good Boys*, a 2019 comedy from producer Seth Rogan. The movie starred Jacob Tremblay, Keith Williams, and Brady Noon as three sixth graders who encounter Kitty and believe her to be a dummy used for CPR training.

A Pipedream representative said at the time: "The buzz from *Good Boys* is spreading fast. We love that Kitty also appears in the film trailer, which allows consumers to see her lifelike face and body without having to head to the theatre."

But when it comes to movies promoting the sale of sex toys – and BDSM accessories in particular – the one with the biggest 'impact' was *Fifty Shades of Grey*. Released the day before Valentine's Day 2015, just about every mainstream TV channel highlighted it somewhere in their schedule in the week before launch, and there could not have been a national or regional newspaper which did not run a related piece or six.

On 3rd February, a full two weeks before the movie's release, ITV's *This Morning* daytime magazine show did its bit to prep the nation. The programme featured a segment called 'Bondage for Beginners' in the company of guest Annabelle Knight, which included instructional demonstrations by scantily clad models, along with quite candid reviews of products. Presenter Phillip Schofield trying out a nipple clamp was a particular highlight.

Twitter, rather predictably, went nuts, with the hashtag #bondageforbeginners attracting comments such as, "Looks like #fetish just went mainstream on @itvthismorning" and "I was just thinking that morning TV is lacking a bondage tutorial". It did not take long for adult firms to begin plugging their own products with the hashtag, nor did it take long for a backlash. Ofcom received 70 complaints about the segment and Mediawatch-UK said the programme had set a dangerous example.

The following week on BBC2, Charlie Brooker devoted a significant portion of his *Weekly Wipe* to the movie, which he described as "an erotic beat 'em up starring a Lego version of Colin Firth" and the next day Ann Summers CEO Jacqueline Gold was invited on to afternoon gripe-fest *Loose Women* to talk about *FSoG*. Star Jamie Dornan turned up on BBC1's *Graham Norton Show* the same day, as part of the movie's promotional tour.

Movies are routinely launched every week, and stars are trotted out to appear on magazine-type shows to plug the product as a matter of course, but it rapidly became apparent that this launch was turning into a genuine event.

Innis & Gunn, a Scottish brewery, created a limited-edition beer made with aphrodisiac ingredients called Fifty Shades of Green. It was blended with 50 different types of hops from around the world, and infused with ginseng, which is said to boost sexual desire. A bargain at £30 a bottle.

London Fire Brigade announced that it was braced for an increase in callouts from people getting stuck or trapped in objects such as handcuffs or cock rings. It said that the number of such incidents had increased year on year since publication of the book so it launched a campaign called Fifty Shades of Red, asking people to think carefully before getting themselves into sticky situations.

It cited examples such as the man who was forced to undergo surgery to remove two metal rings that had been stuck on his penis for three days. He had visited A&E in a London hospital but, when doctors couldn't remove them, two firefighters were required to scrub up and cut them off with hydraulic cutting equipment. Another unfortunate chap got his todger stuck in a toaster, and yet another in a vacuum cleaner.

Although this all made for good copy, the costs of attending such incidents had topped £400,000 over three years, with each callout costing taxpayers at least £295. Third Officer Dave Brown said: "The Fifty Shades effect seems to spike handcuff incidents so we hope film goers will use common sense and avoid leaving themselves red faced."

The Women's Institute became linked to the movie after a headline in *The Telegraph* said: 'One doesn't expect this smut! The X-rated bodice ripper that makes Fifty Shades sound tame... written by the WI.' The facts were rather less interesting, however. Wellington WI writing club had published a short-run compilation of stories written by members in order to raise funds for a cancer charity and among the fiction and poetry was a story called 'The Conquering Gibraltarian Adonis', which came with an 18-plus warning.

The three-page story, about a couple called Mariah and Clive, featured a romp on kitchen worktops and included the lines: 'his balls were throbbing', 'his huge penis was engorged', and 'he put his arms around her waist from behind and gently gyrated his massive schlong against her lovely wide buttocks'. The identity of the author was kept secret and the writer who ran the group said: "She doesn't want anyone to know it was her. She said her gran would be furious."

Adult dating website *MaritalAffair.co.uk* reported a 110% increase in membership enquiries. "Interest in fantasy-based sex is growing and the great British public are casting off the uptight sexual attitude they were once infamous for," the company said. "Many Britons now treat sex as a hobby, and the prudish image they once had is quickly becoming a thing of the past."

Bright Day, a UK-based online dating provider running over 350 matchmaking sites, reported greater interest in categories such as BDSM-lovers and those seeking wealthy men. Having analysed 10,000 of the sites' dating profiles, Bright Day founder Andy Hammonds said: "A few years ago, our more 'adult' dating sites were doing okay but were only visited by a handful of people who had enjoyed an alternative lifestyle in the bedroom for some time. Since *Fifty Shades of Grey* however, we've seen an 11% increase in BDSM-focused dating sites to meet the demand from members who are exploring their kinky sides for the very first time."

Bright Day's sites targeting the 'sugar daddy' niche had also seen an 8% rise since 2012. "*Fifty Shades of Grey* has been a game-changer for the online dating industry," Hammonds said. "It's made certain lifestyles far more mainstream. If people are looking for partners online and can choose the height and location of their ideal match, why not be specific about tastes in the bedroom?"

But *IllicitEncounters.com*, the dating site for married people who want an affair, said its research indicated the British were all talk. A survey of 2,500 people conducted by the site found that having a threesome was the number one male fantasy, but 80% of people wouldn't want to actually take part in one. And, rather surprisingly, only 48% of men and 46% of women would be willing to have sex with the lights on.

32% said they had read the books and although 74% were interested in exploring some of the scenes and ideas from the trilogy, a whopping 89% said they would never feel comfortable requesting anything other than the norm in the bedroom from their partner.

"This is exactly why people come to us, to get better sex!" the company's Claire Page said. "There are more than a few real-life Christian Greys on our site: the average guy on IE is statistically more successful, wealthy, and well-educated than your typical British man with the budget for our membership. However, our ladies seem to be a bit more empowered than the protagonist Ana, and more willing to ask for what they want, even in their actual profiles."

Rhi Kemp-Davies, a sex toy consultant from Cardiff, told *Wales Online*: "Some people think that since *Fifty Shades* came out, they can talk about these things a bit more. It's so mainstream there's no shame in talking about things like that because everyone is. That makes it 'safe'."

The Mirror reported that a woman from Devon had set up an eBay business for the shy. For a fiver a time, she would write "almost anything" in a *Fifty Shades*-style raunchy letter to a customer's secret crush and she said that she had been inundated with requests. "I think people need that extra little push to give them the confidence to admit that they like this saucier side of things," she was quoted as saying. "And there are loads of girls and boys out there who probably want to send something a little more risqué to their loved one but are just too shy or feel uncomfortable writing something like that – or they might not know how."

Olympian Louise Hazel, a fan of the books, devised a *FSoG*-inspired exercise workout featuring ropes, chain, and pain and even posed nude to promote it. The 45-minute high-intensity workout was designed to shed body fat fast and she claimed the classes would leave people feeling orgasmic. She told *MailOnline*: "The workout is designed to kick-start and ignite your desire to exercise which, like sex, releases feel-good hormones called endorphins. It will empower you, it will challenge you, and you'll beg for mercy. However, I guarantee that you'll feel amazing afterwards."

The always-opportunistic bookmakers Paddy Power reportedly offered a series of special bets surrounding the release of the film, such as Anastasia being the top baby girls' name and Christian to be the top baby boys' name in 2015 (20/1 and 25/1 respectively) and restaurant chain TGI Friday's created a special limited-edition cocktail called Mr Grey Screaming Orgasm to mark the launch of the movie.

For those who wanted more than just a taste of the Grey lifestyle, a number of hotels were promoting *Fifty Shades*-themed weekend Valentine packages, with Seattle's Edgewater Hotel's offering including a helicopter tour and the use of an Audi R8 Spyder during guests' stay, and perhaps the least convincing cash-in came from Unilever, which introduced a 'sexy' campaign for its Surf laundry detergent called Flirty Shades of Surf.

Retailers of adult products had known for months when the movie was landing so they had plenty of time to prepare for it and make mutually beneficial arrangements with companies in other sectors. Some created installations in cinema foyers and Vibez Adult Boutique of Aylesford in Kent went further, producing a 30-second cinema advertisement which was shown during screenings of the movie and also creating a Red Room in-store to showcase the products featured.

Many other retailers ran *FSoG*-themed promotions, including Pulse & Cocktails, which offered a 20% discount to customers who brought their cinema tickets with them after seeing the film. Even Amazon started shoving sex toys in its customers' faces, highlighting lines such as Fetish Fantasy Series Pleasure Tape, Cheeky Weekender Love Affair Kit, and vibes by Cascade, Lelo, Rocks-Off, and PicoBong in its daily Lightning Deals.

Online retailer JD Williams ran a rather clever 'Over 50 Shades of Grey' campaign, aimed at mature women, which featured three silver foxes posing in their underwear. "We can expect to be bombarded with images of young women looking luscious in lingerie at this time of year, but what about the more mature woman?" commented Carie Barkhuizen, JD Williams spokesperson. "Our research discovered that 52% of UK women feel most confident aged 45+, so what better way to showcase that confidence [than] by featuring mature models aged 50+ looking just as fantastic – and sexy – in lingerie as their younger counterparts?"

As regional media rarely covered the business of pleasure, several local newspapers appeared stuck for someone to provide quotes to pad out their reports, so they turned to Ann Summers' managers on their patch. The Carlisle branch manager told *The Cumbria News & Star*: "Since the *Fifty Shades of Grey* hype we've seen a huge rise in sales in our erotic lingerie lines including cami suspenders, lace bodies and Sexcessories. Red fluffy handcuffs and massage oils in particular have been flying off the shelves and there has been an increased interest in couples' toys."

A spokesperson the chain's Gloucester branch told *The Gloucester Citizen*: "Handcuffs are our biggest sellers. They've been flying off the shelves. Whips, paddles, blindfolds, and nipple tassels are all doing quite a lot better too. We have had a lot more people coming in and asking about things they probably wouldn't normally."

The Middlesbrough store manager said: "There has definitely been a heightened interest in bondage-esque products from our customers throughout the past few months...We're also finding that our customers are asking more questions about our Sexcessories and we hope that the film will help open the eyes and minds of those who were previously a little shy about experimenting in the bedroom."

In the same report, Ann Summers said that it had received more than double the usual number of party planner applications from the Teeside area.

Perhaps the most unexpected retailer to clamber aboard the *Fifty Shades* bandwagon was B&Q. A leaked staff memo from the DIY chain warned its staff that rope, cable ties, and duct tape may be bought in large numbers by customers outside of the store's usual demographic. The memo said that after the publication of the books in 2012 it experienced, 'increased demand of certain products and queries from customers as they tried to recreate their own *Fifty Shades* experiences' and it added: 'We need to be prepared for the same effect when the film is released'. It went on to suggest that staff should familiarise themselves with the book and head office would duly be sending copies to stores for this purpose.

The memo was taken at face value by *The Guardian, The Mirror, The Daily Mail* and the UK Press Association but B&Q said in a statement a few days later: "We can confirm that the leaked memo was indeed a bit of fun. B&Q, the public and the media have been entertained over the past few days and we are looking forward to a big weekend. We would have confessed to this sooner, but our hands were tied."

As for the movie itself, the signs weren't promising. British director Sam Taylor-Johnson admitted there were numerous creative differences between her and author EL James during production and there were rumours that the two leading actors didn't actually get on.

Reviews started appearing on IMDb as early as the 10th of February and there were some very harsh words to be found in the Most Useful posts.

Sarangi2015 from Australia said: "This movie is atrocious beyond words... The script was laughable. No chemistry between the two leads. As for the 'eroticism' it was completely lacking. Stilted, awkward, poor cinematography, cheesy scripting. Just terrible."

Westeire from Ireland said: "Lacks any of the raunch or controversy promised, and is instead tiresome, banal and as thinly plotted as a porn... If a man had written the book he would probably have been jailed."

Some professional UK critics were almost as scathing, with Peter Bradshaw in *The Guardian* giving it one star and saying the performances of its two leads were "strictly daytime soap". *The Daily Beast* said that the only other time sex had looked so choreographed in a movie was in *Team America* – a satirical comedy starring puppets.

The cinema-going public weren't listening though, and entire multi-screen complexes were taken over by *Fifty Shades of Grey*, with huge queues forming outside and showings starting every thirty minutes at my local.

Despite the unprecedented crowds, I only heard of police being called to one screening, which took place in Glasgow. A man reportedly asked a group of three drunk women to keep the noise down and they responded by glassing him.

Fifty Shades of Grey chalked up the UK's highest ever box office opening for an 18-rated film, taking £4.6m on Friday the 13th alone. In the US its numbers were even more impressive: it took $81.7m, making it the highest grossing Presidents Day Weekend opener and one of the biggest R-rated debuts in history. It was also New Zealand's most successful R-rated debut and the biggest ever movie release in South Africa. In total, internationally, it earned $239m during its opening weekend, repaying its $40m budget more than handsomely.

Cinema chains had another reason to thank EL James. The movie helped them sell a record number of ad slots and even brought in some upmarket new advertisers, including Calvin Klein Jeans, Estée Lauder, and Nike. Karen Stacey, CEO of Digital Cinema Media in the UK, said: "We've seen a huge amount of interest from a wide range of female-focused brands looking to book into *Fifty Shades of Grey*. It's set to be one of the most talked-about films of 2015 and these brands have all recognised the opportunity on offer to engage with the young, upmarket, early-adopting, social media savvy audience the film is set to attract."

While *FSoG* was always going to carry an 18-rating in the UK, the French were clearly unimpressed with its raunchy content and – probably after an indifferent shrug – gave it a 12-rating, the country's second lowest certification. The president of France's Board of Film Classification described *Fifty Shades* as a "schmaltzy romance" and "not a film that can shock a lot of people". Italy gave it a 14, the Czech Republic and Sweden considered it a 15, the Netherlands, Iceland, and Spain a 16, while Thailand thought it a 20.

In the US, Sportsheets, the brand behind the Sex & Mischief range of BDSM accessories, held a private screening of the film for its staff, local customers, and press. "We love seeing how much the books have done for our business and our demographic of customers," said Julie Stewart, company president. "We saw a huge surge in sales when the books came out. We're very excited about the consumer response to the movie release and how it will increase our business again."

Pipedream's Icicles products were featured in a *Newsweek Special Edition* devoted to *Fifty Shades* and the firm also popped up on CNN, when the cable news channel ran a segment featuring the manufacturer's Fetish Fantasy Limited Edition Bondage Rope, Bondage Tape, and Fetish Fantasy Gold Ball Gag and Collar & Leash.

There was inevitably a backlash, and it started the week before, when it emerged that a woman from California had launched a class action lawsuit against author EL James and Lovehoney because her officially licensed lube failed to live up to her expectations. The bottle stated that users would 'experience enhanced orgasms and stimulation as every tingle, touch and vibration intensifies' but she apparently didn't get that, despite buying the product on at least two occasions. Although not in any way relevant to the movie, the media reported the story with a certain glee.

More seriously, domestic violence campaigners called for a boycott of the movie, as did the odd religious leader, with one archbishop describing it as a "direct assault on Christian marriage", while a group called Fifty Shades Is Domestic Abuse protested outside the London premiere, saying the novel dangerously romanticised the idea that women can fix broken men.

Mediawatch-UK said on its blog: 'Valentine's Day, more usually associated with flowers, chocolate and romance is, this year, being hijacked as a promotional vehicle for the release of the film *Fifty Shades of Grey*... The book on which this film was based glamorised and legitimised both sexual and domestic violence. With the mainstream release and promotion of this film, opinion makers, the media and celebrities are legitimising this violence too... The extended trailer for the film calls it a 'fairy tale'; a misleading description which suggests a simple love story and masks the film's true themes of humiliation, manipulation, abuse, and degradation of women. The 'fairy tale' in this film is that, in reality, women in relationships such as the one depicted in the film don't end up like Anastasia: they often end up in a woman's shelter, on the run for years, or dead."

In the US, Texas megachurch pastor Ed Young said: "The book *Fifty Shades of Grey* is a perverted attempt to trap readers and leads them to a misunderstanding of what intimacy and connection are all about. It is a pathetic distortion of a more powerful reality about relationships. God is not anti-sex, and he isn't grey when it comes to relationships. I want to wake people up to the reality that God's purpose and plan for their lives is so much greater!"

Pastor Ed was planning to 'baptize' copies of the books during a sermon tied to the release of his own title, called (I promise I'm not making this up) *Fifty Shades of They*. Based on biblical standards and the teaching of pastor Ed, the book contained 'Fifty simple, yet profound insights that will help any relationship thrive, from friendships to business partnerships to marriages'.

In a similar vein, US authors Dr Juli Slattery and Dannah K Gresh were offering free copies of their title, *Pulling Back the Shades: Erotica, Intimacy, and the Longings of a Woman's Heart,* to women who traded in their copies of *Fifty Shades of Grey*.

"*Pulling Back the Shades* addresses God's design for intimacy and shows why erotica is exploiting women's longings rather than satisfying them," Slattery and Gresh said.

Even Amanda Taylor, MD of UK fetish fashionistas Honour, criticised it for misrepresenting bondage and fetish fashion: "Our gentle art faces an image predicament with the arrival of the film," she said. "We're liberated and empowered by the sensation of metering out our careful, mutually beneficial, bondage roleplay and the film jeopardises that."

The media went all-in on its coverage. *Mail Online* featured the Official Pleasure Collection in dozens of its contemporary news articles, and *The Telegraph* also featured the collection in its 'Valentine's Day Gift Guide', describing the range as the tools 'to take your erotic awakening from the page to the bedroom', while the *London Evening Standard* showcased the official products in its 'Fifty Shades of Pleasure' guide, describing them as the best toys to 'let your *Fifty Shades of Grey* fantasies come to life'. *Now Magazine* told its 2.5 million readers that the items in the Official Pleasure Collection were 'the best-selling sex toys in the UK since they launched'.

In the US, NBC's *Access Hollywood Live* featured the range in a two-minute 'Fifty Shades for Rookies' segment telling viewers how to give their Valentine's date night a 'Fifty Shades of Pleasure' make-over, while CBS's *The Insider* explored how couples could recreate what they see on screen in Christian Grey's Red Room using the collection.

CNBC's 'Fifty Shades of Green' report revealed how retailers were preparing to cash-in on the release of the movie by selling the officially licensed products and HBO's *Last Week Tonight* with John Oliver took a sideways look at the phenomenon and featured the collection's You Are Mine Metal Handcuffs. After broadcast on HBO, the clip was subsequently viewed 1.5 million times on *YouTube*.

The US business press also highlighted the boost the Official Pleasure Collection would give to adult retailers. "Purveyors of official merchandise are already experiencing a rush of demand," said *Bloomberg* in an article syndicated worldwide, describing *Fifty Shades of Grey* as "a recognisable brand for the mass population".

'*Fifty Shades of Grey* in sales frenzy,' ran the headline in *The Hollywood Reporter*. "Now that the movie is arriving, merchandise numbers likely will hit new heights," the article said. *The New York Times*, Fox21News, and *Nasdaq.com* also featured the Official Pleasure Collection.

Europe's most watched television channel, TF1, featured a number of Official Pleasure Collection items online in its selection of Valentine's Day essentials and even *Buzzfeed* got involved, using the items from the collection to try bondage play for the first time.

Lovehoney co-founder Richard Longhurst said: "The coverage that The Official Pleasure Collection has received from mainstream media is phenomenal. No pleasure industry brand has ever received this level of coverage."

Nor sold like it. Sales of the collection, which included sex toys not seen in the movie, were spectacular, as were sales of similar products to those brandished by Mr Grey. Lovehoney had its biggest ever week in the run up to the movie's release, with orders being received every three seconds at one point, and the week following release saw sales of bondage gear increase by 80%.

"We have enjoyed the perfect storm of Valentine's Day coming at the same time as the biggest erotic movie of all time," said Longhurst. "The media hype has been remarkable but what is more important is that the hype is being reflected at the box office. Millions of people are going to see the movie and then looking to experiment with BDSM afterwards. The movie is a great advertisement for the pleasure that you can enjoy through BDSM."

Some unlikely names joined the party, with an Official Pleasure Collection pop-up shop opening in the iconic Fenwick department store on Bond Street, in the heart of Mayfair, and the queen of the scene, author EL James, was the guest of honour at the launch of a luxury collection of bondage gear at Coco de Mer in London's Covent Garden.

For retailers of adult products, 2015 was a year to remember, and the following year saw two more Official Collections launched, in anticipation of the 2017 release of the *Fifty Shades Darker* movie. When it did hit the big screen, the critics liked it even less than its predecessor. Giving it just one star, Brian Viner in *The Daily Mail* called it: "Fifty shades duller! And as erotic as a bluebottle landing on your bottom."

Catherine Shoard, writing in *The Guardian*, also gave it one star and said: "Submissive sequel offers little light relief but lots of washing."

The Independent's Geoffrey Macnab was also in the one-star club. He said: "*Fifty Shades Darker* is an ordeal to watch not because of its gothic eroticism but because of its utter blandness."

The Telegraph film critic, Robbie Collin, awarded it two stars and said: "It's an alleged 18-rated, adults-only filth-fest that behaves like a flustered PG."

It spawned some fun headlines though. 'Who Keeps Bringing All These Vegetables to Fifty Shades Screenings?' was seen on the *Cosmopolitan* website. The piece cited instances of abandoned cucumbers being found on cinema floors after screenings of the movie.

Fifty Shades Freed, the final episode of the trilogy, arrived in movie theatres in February 2018 and once again there were official collections of branded toys to capitalise on the publicity that surrounded it. *Fifty Shades Freed* was the lowest-grossing film of the three and, like its two predecessors, it did not find favour with the critics. But also like its predecessors, it did help to move a lot of sex toys.

"While this might seem to be a 'good' problem to have for PR purposes – 'The show was so popular we had to turn people away, darling!' – it was anything but 'good' for those queuing outside in the rain, who had been told they could only enter when other visitors had left."

You might be surprised how many hobbies, pastimes, and areas of interest have annual events dedicated to them, where visitors can meet up with fellow enthusiasts, attend presentations, peruse the wares of suppliers which service the sector, and leave with carrier bags stuffed full of flyers and branded merch.

In addition to events with fairly widespread appeal, such as the BBC Good Food Show, the Horse of the Year Show, MCM Comic Con, and the National Franchise Exhibition, the last quarter of 2022 saw the UK's National Exhibition Centre (NEC) host Euro Bus Expo, Lab Innovations, Saltex (turf management), and Spie Photonex (sciences, techniques, and products that generate, transmit, process and capture light of all types).

There were also shows dedicated to art & antiques, cakes, Christmas parties, classic cars, dogs, farming, model railways, motorcycles, recruitment, snow, wellbeing and many more areas of interest.

Details of these and other events can be found on the venue's website, but you will search in vain for an exhibition where sellers of sex toys showcase their latest launches. This might come as a surprise if you remember the glory days of Erotica – that's the adult lifestyle consumer show, not the 1992 Madonna album.

The first Erotica event was held at London's Olympia in November 1997, where it returned every year until 2012. Olympia, a Victorian complex of vast halls in West Kensington, opened in 1886 and it has staged everything from a mass meeting of Sir Oswald Mosley's British Union of Fascists in 1934 to Ru Paul's DragCon UK in 2020. It has also staged a Miss World pageant, a Jimi Hendrix concert, and several Chris Eubank boxing matches, but its day job is hosting exhibitions, and its grand architecture and ambience of faded elegance was perfect for Erotica.

Exhibitors were located in themed areas. Photographers, artists and sculptors were grouped together, as were suppliers of BDSM furniture and equipment, fetish clothing, lingerie, sex toys, and DVDs, and dominating the main hall was the stage, where burlesque-style performances ran several times each day.

Mingling with the crowds and adding to the atmosphere were entertainers, including a mobile-organ-playing comedy nun, and the odd person in a Masked Singer-style costume promoting worthy causes (such as a giant pair of walking hairy testicles highlighting *MaleCancer.net* one year).

At its peak, the organisers claimed Erotica attracted more visitors than The Ideal Home Exhibition, and although the actual attendance figures were never published, I was present several times when the doors had to be closed as Olympia was at its maximum capacity.

In an industry starved of a public-facing shop window, no supplier of erotic goods wishing to raise its profile, increase its mailing list, or turn surplus stock into cash, could afford to miss Erotica. It was marketed as an adult lifestyle event, so its showguides were packed with pictures of corsets, latex fetishwear, tasteful erotic gifts, and desirable artisan jewellery.

The relatively high price of admission (£19.50 per person back in 2002) encouraged visitors to open their wallets and buy from exhibitors, so they at least left with something to commemorate their visit, as photography was strictly prohibited.

And the number of exhibitors was always in three figures. Looking for a swinging holiday in an exotic location? A pair of ballet-style ankle boots with 7" heels? A life-size bronze sculpture of an unfulfilled woman using a flame cutter to create her ideal man? You'd find it at Erotica.

Erotica was welcoming to all, regardless of sexual orientation, and a safe space for visitors to dress as they pleased, with no fear of judgement. And as well as funding the on-site security team, perhaps the high entry price also ensured that only people who genuinely wanted to attend were there, as I never witnessed any groups of drunks causing trouble.

I did see representatives of the media, however, and Erotica enjoyed plenty of coverage over the years, particularly if a celeb was appearing or performing the ceremonial cutting of the ribbon to open the show. An inventor of a quirky product could take a small stand at Erotica on the Friday and find themselves in the following Sunday's newspapers if what they were showing caught the right eye.

It all sounds rather wonderful, doesn't it? So why isn't it still taking place?

The organisers couldn't be accused of complacency. In a bid to expand into other territories, Erotica attempted to franchise the concept overseas and in March 2003 London Erotica was joined by a sister event at Manchester's G-Mex Centre.

Despite being identical in concept, the northern show failed to attract the same number of exhibitors or visitors. Contributing to the lack of the latter was the steep ticket price (£25 for Saturday admission) and the lack of support the event received from the local media.

Inviting Neil and Christine Hamilton to officially open the show the following year did bring the press out – I was one of about a dozen photographers snapping them cavorting with some of the stage performers outside the building – but visitor numbers were again disappointing, even though it was promoted on BBC Northwest, and radio stations Galaxy FM and TalkSport.

When the 2005 event was about to open, the organisers told *The Manchester Evening News* that it may be the last one to be staged in the north, due to the low number of visitors: "We thought Manchester was a sexy city, but perhaps we were wrong," said an Erotica spokesperson. "Ironically, more women from the north head to our November event at London's Olympia than are prepared to be seen having fun in their own city. Our research has shown that they are intimidated by their men, who don't want their inadequacies exposed. We thought that Manchester had entered the 21st Century like everywhere else, but it seems Mancunians in particular are stuck in the past."

After the story hit the website of *The Manchester Evening News*, it drew a largely hostile response in the comments section, even from one chap who enjoyed the show: "Let's blame it on a generalised view that the male population in the north all hold the same views on sex and expression, not the fact that little advertising was distributed and that it is a young exhibition compared to the capital's," he said. "I did attend and found it to be a very interesting and eye-opening activity. I would definitely recommend it to people...Word of mouth works but takes time, and slagging off the whole population of the north is not a way to publicise an event."

This same point was made by another poster: "If the organiser wants to encourage people to go to the show, maybe insulting them and their city is not the best way to go about it."

You might not be surprised to learn that 2005's was indeed the last Erotica to be held in Manchester.

Erotica events in the early noughties also had trade sections, where retailers could meet up with their suppliers, slightly apart from the crowds and the bustle of the show floor. However, the exuberant hollering from stage shows and PA systems was hardly conducive to doing business, with conversations often having to be held in raised voices. So when a dedicated B2B event was launched at the NEC in the summer of 2005, with no stage shows, and no general public, some exhibitors switched allegiance to it.

Erotica was still a fantastic consumer event though, and 2005's London show was the biggest so far, with the gallery level opened up for the first time and over 220 exhibitors listed in the showguide. As if meeting all these suppliers under one roof on the same day wasn't enough, Erotica's timing – the third week of November – was perfect for people shopping for gifts, especially if they were looking for something unavailable in mainstream outlets.

The show's location, so close to Kensington High Street, with its selection of eateries and bars was another plus, and venturing outside of the local area, visitors making a weekend of it could take in a show or flash their cash in London's most upmarket shops. And for those who still wanted more sexiness after Erotica had closed, there was the Erotica Ball at a top London nightclub, which featured performers from Erotica's stage show.

In anticipation of the London show visitor count continuing to increase, the organisers added an extra day to the three-day show calendar in 2005. The aim was to spread the number of attendees out and avoid the Grand Hall being closed because it had reached capacity, which had happened in both 2003 and 2004. While this might seem to be a 'good' problem to have for PR purposes – "The show was so popular we had to turn people away, darling!" – it was anything but 'good' for those queuing outside in the rain, who had been told they could only enter when other visitors had left.

But, as is often the way, bigger did not necessarily mean better. There were more stands in 2005 but not all of them had an obvious erotic connection. Joining 'the regulars' were firms promoting confectionary, beauty treatments, spa baths, hair extensions, and even vegetarianism. Exhibitor Dominic Hawes, of sex toy brand Mantric Marketing, told our reporter: "It's a lot less fetishy and more high street than previous years, and has slightly lost the carnival atmosphere that it used to have."

The grumbles continued after the show and into 2006, when a group of disgruntled exhibitors set up an egroup called EEFABS (Erotica Exhibitors for a Better Show) so opinions could be voiced and shared. According to EEFABS, 2005's event was a big disappointment with takings down by as much as 30% on the previous year, despite the extra day of trading.

It was unclear whether this was due to the visitor spend being shared among more stands or whether the actual number of visitors was down on 2004. EEFABS members were also unhappy with the large number of non-erotic exhibitors and the news that stand prices would be rising 20% for 2006.

After initially rebutting the complaints, the Erotica organisers eventually came up with a revised package for 2006, but EEFABS still had concerns. A spokesperson for the group commented: "Some of the changes are welcome, such as a step back from the drastic price increases and a four-day show, and they have now introduced smaller and lower cost stands which is a move in the right direction. However, Erotica have not addressed many other concerns such as what should constitute suitable types of exhibitors in order to keep the show 'erotic' and the need for more investment into the show by way of new features and attractions."

It was all a bit awkward, and there were fewer exhibitors at 2006's event even though the organisers pushed the boat out with the stage show, which included performances from American burlesque star Dita Von Teese.

It was more of the same in 2007, including Dita, but by 2008 the UK was in the grip of recession, and there were several notable absences from the exhibitor listings, and fewer again in 2009.

The 2010 show was promoted with 30-second adverts on Channel 4, a first for the event, and it seemed to pay off, with more than one old timer telling our reporter it was the best Erotica they'd experienced in terms of sales, but the 2011 incarnation showed signs of a downturn, with wider aisles resulting from less stands. Also, the entry price was higher – £30 on Saturday – and the stage show was shorter.

2011 was the first year visitors were permitted to take photographs inside the hall. In the early days this policy protected the privacy of attendees, but we were well on the way to becoming a social media society by this time, and Erotica had missed out on several years of 'free' publicity generated from visitors' sharing their experiences online, which might have widened the event's appeal.

There were rumours that the show would move to a smaller hall for 2012, but what actually happened was far worse: the organisers announced that Erotica 2012 had been cancelled.

The cost of a tenancy at London's Olympia rose every year in line with the Retail Price Index and the organisers said that it would have been difficult to run the event without either further increasing the price of entry tickets or charging exhibitors significantly more than they had paid previously. The show would return in 2013, with a 'new generation' format, possibly in a different venue.

Of all the years for Erotica to miss, 2012 was the most unfortunate, with Fifty Shades Fever arriving in the summer. With that as its backdrop, Erotica would surely have been packed to the rafters with visitors and media, but there was no way for the organisers to know that in April, when the decision was made to pull the plug on the event.

Erotica did return in 2013 at a different venue: East London's Tobacco Dock. Built in 1812 as a warehouse for imported tobacco, it was launched as an events and conference space in 2012, with a capacity for up to 10,000 visitors. The change of location allowed organisers to reduce prices for both exhibitors and visitors and marketing included a fleet of the capital's taxis being wrapped in Erotica branding.

It took place a month earlier than previous events and was officially opened by cast members of MTV reality series *Geordie Shore*. It appeared to be a success, with organisers and exhibitors alike declaring themselves pleased with the new format, but in February 2014 it emerged that plans for that year's event had been cancelled.

And that was the end of Erotica. It wasn't perfect but for most of its life it was the best shop window the UK adult sector had. It allowed many small businesses to grow and flourish and served as a focal point for media coverage of all things sexy.

Over the years there had been others seeking to grab a slice of Erotica's pie. The early noughties saw the 18+ Show in Brighton and Festival Erotique in Edinburgh, which both ran for two years and were managed by local entrepreneurs with industry connections. Long running regional fetish-themed events, such as London Alternative Market and Birmingham Bizarre Bazaar, continue to be staged today but that sector's flagship show was the Skin Two Expo, and this too came to a sad end.

All had seemed to be well with the event until 2007, when the show sponsor (*Skin Two* magazine) fell out with the show organiser (Green Shed Events). Instead of settling their differences, the two parties decided to stage competing shows.

The new show, run by the old team at the old location in the Barbican Centre, had a new name (The Xpo) while the old show (*Skin Two* Expo) was run by a new team at a new location at ExCeL in Docklands, under the old name.

As if that wasn't confusing enough for exhibitors and visitors, both events were held in London on the same two days: Friday the 5th and Saturday the 6th of October 2007.

Neither show returned the following year.

Also competing for visitors on that same October 2007 weekend was the brand-new Adults Only Show at Birmingham's National Indoor Arena. The marketing campaign looked impressive, with local and national radio and print advertising, media partnerships with leading adult-themed magazines, and outdoor advertising. Plus 40,000 flyers and 15,000 branded condoms were scheduled to be distributed to local pubs and clubs.

Like Erotica, Adults Only Show offered visitors a mix of live stage performances and shopping opportunities, though its debut event only attracted just over 70 exhibitors. Visitor numbers were also disappointing, with around 7,400 people passing through the doors during the show's three-day duration.

A remarkably similar number of visitors (7,500) was claimed for the inaugural Passion event, which took place at Earls Court over the May 2008 bank holiday weekend, despite the organisers appearing to do everything that could reasonably be expected of them.

Neither Adults Only Show nor Passion returned to the industry calendar after their debut years, allowing Erotica to retain its monopoly status on national exhibitions in the UK for the remainder of its life. But when it was revealed that there would be no 2014 Erotica, two new consumer events were announced for the following year: Sexhibition and Sexpo UK.

Sexhibition certainly looked the part, with giant illuminated letters spelling out the name of the event on stage and forming an excellent backdrop to photographs. It was held at Manchester's Event City on August 22nd and 23rd and the general consensus was it had a successful launch.

The Sexhibition organisers were new to large scale events, but Sexpo UK was a licensed version of an established overseas show, so the UK-based organisers had a successful template to follow. The first Sexpo was held in Australia in 1996 and it ran several times a year in different cities. It had also been successful in South Africa, and everything looked set for the UK incarnation to establish itself as a replacement for Erotica: it was even held at Olympia in mid-November.

As the doors opened on its first day – Friday 13th November 2015 – hopes were high for a bumper attendance over the weekend but that evening there came shocking news from Paris. Gunmen and suicide bombers attacked a concert hall, a stadium, restaurants, and bars, leaving 130 people dead and hundreds wounded.

Unsurprisingly, spending a weekend in a major European capital no longer held the same appeal as it had the previous week, and attendance at Sexpo UK – just under 10,000 – was significantly less than expected. Even some people who had bought tickets in advance chose to stay away.

The licensees chose not to exercise their option to run the event the following year, giving Sexhibition the opportunity to establish itself as the UK's flagship show. Sexhibition's sophomore event was moved to Manchester's Victoria Warehouse and appeared to be even more successful than its predecessor, with organisers announcing that not only had they committed to five more years at the venue, but they were also looking at hosting a London version.

There were a few grumbles however, which Sexhibition co-organiser Cheryl Smith addressed when she spoke to *ETO*'s reporter: "We've taken an event that was one year in and dropped it into a new venue, with all the pros and cons that come with that," she said. "Essentially, without 2015's template to follow, it's felt like creating the event from scratch again... I can't pretend it's been an easy ride. It's not. Organising large events is horrible in many ways and it's been immensely stressful. It's a small team doing a lot, without years of experience, so it's relentless."

However, she concluded: "I'm proud we've stuck with it, and of the show we've delivered again."

But there were to be no more Sexhibitions, in Manchester nor London, and once again the UK was without a consumer show, although it came close on two more occasions. In March 2019 Sexpo founder David Ross announced that he had taken responsibility for the running of UK events, and the first would be in July at the NEC.

In May it emerged that the show would be taking place in October rather than July, as a result of licensing issues with the local council, caused by the organisers being non-UK residents. And two months later, another show was pencilled into industry wallplanners: scheduled for the first week of May 2020, Expo Erotica – no relation to the previous Erotica – was the brainchild of Inger Stevenson, whose background was in events management.

"I've always wanted to put together a show like this and the time just seemed right," she told *ETO*. "I feel that this is a very undervalued industry in terms of how it's generally perceived and by doing Expo Erotica we can raise the bar and at the same time reach a new customer base."

Neither event took place. Eight days before the doors of Sexpo UK were due to open, the show was cancelled completely, following a dispute with its ticketing partner, according to the show's website. And two months before Expo Erotica was due to be held, prime minister Boris Johnson put the UK into lockdown to stop the spread of COVID-19.

With the rather chaotic recent history of UK consumer shows, sex toy brands have turned to other 'events' to help them get the public's attention. The build-up to 14th February is the most obvious one but Sexual Health Week (observed from the second full Monday to Sunday in September) has also proven productive to piggyback press releases onto.

But every day in the calendar is 'special'. Or, more accurately, every single day of the year has been appropriated to garner publicity for a certain agenda, and many of them are burdened with multiple labels. Take 1st of January for example. Not only is it National Hangover Day, which is perfectly understandable, but it's also Global Family Day, Public

Domain Day, National First Foot Day, Apple Gifting Day, World Day of Peace, National Bloody Mary Day, Z Day, Ring a Bell Day, Copyright Law Day, Euro Day, Commitment Day, and Polar Bear Plunge Day.

You're right, it does sound a load of bollocks, but the mainstream media is always looking for frothy fluff. Much of its main news is so depressing, and a decent designated 'day' can not only help to fill column inches but also bump up page views and maybe even increase ad spend.

There is a National Sex Toy Day (4th of November) and others with potential for brands to exploit in their marketing include Satisfied Staying Single Day, Handcuff Day, Check Your Batteries Day, and National Massage Day.

Maybe because it's in the middle of summer, when news tends to be slow, but a particularly popular 'day' for sex toy suppliers has been National Orgasm Day (NOD) on 31st of July.

2014 proved to be a vintage year for NOD: on social media, Lovehoney offered a Deluxe Magic Wand in a follow and retweet campaign, and also put together a 'Ten Top Tips for Better Orgasms' piece; Sextoys.co.uk promoted a special one-day-only discount code to its followers; Simply Pleasure highlighted its G-spot vibrators; Nice 'n' Naughty offered a free gift with every purchase; Bondara ran a competition to win a box of goodies, plus members of its team recounted some of their more memorable sex stories on the company blog; and Ann Summers offered £15 off a selection of sex toys and pointed followers to its *Fifty Shades of Grey*-inspired stats, which also appeared in *The Daily Star*.

In the media, Rebecca Newman wrote a guide to making the most of the day for *The Huffington Post*, *Metro* also went down the guide route, offering readers 15 tips to give them more powerful climaxes, while *The Sun* went one better with 16 suggestions. *The Independent* chose to pen a rather earnest piece, suggesting there might be too much emphasis on 'happy endings' at the expense of intimacy, a theme that was previously explored in a Dr Brooke (formerly known as Belle de Jour) piece in *The Telegraph* the previous year. *The Guardian* offered up a Modern Toss cartoon in advance of the occasion while *The Mirror*'s contribution was a fleshed out version of the Ann Summers survey.

But the star of the day was blogger Cara Sutra. Back in May she co-operated with a journalist who was writing a piece on sex toy testers and wanted a female case study. A syndicated news agency chose the perfect moment to place the story, and *The Daily Mail* was first to run it online, under the heading: 'That's job satisfaction! Woman who works as professional sex toy tester has 15 orgasms at work a week'.

Versions of the story also appeared in *Metro*, *The Mirror*, *The Sun,* and *The Daily Star* and a number of other online media channels. It subsequently spread to Europe, the USA, South America, Australia, and Russia, with Cara's own site experiencing 63k of traffic after it hit Russia.

I'm sure the UK will get another adult-themed consumer show at some point and hopefully the entrepreneur behind it will have thoroughly researched the market in advance. Because while staging an event is relatively straightforward (hire hall, sell space to exhibitors, sell tickets to visitors), staging a successful one, which turns a profit and returns year after year, has proven to be more of a challenge.

"We believe billion-dollar companies will emerge in order to bridge the gap between the underserved sexual and women's healthtech space and the needs of today's society."

The sex toy sector has always been rather frivolous. A bit of a laugh. How could it not be when one considers the intended use of its products? But the second decade of this century witnessed it mature into a genuine industry, taken seriously not just by those who earn their livings in it, but also by outsiders – especially those capable of spotting a bandwagon.

While just about every area of society now sees inclusiveness as desirable and necessary, the sex toy sector was well ahead of that particular curve.

Take Clonezone, for example: back in 1982, four close friends – Mike McCann, Paul Orton, David Edwards, and John Tillyard – formed the company after despairing at the lack of quality products available for the UK gay community. "Paul and I went to the States and basically brought back the basis of the business in suitcases," David Edwards told me in 2004. "We went for a holiday but we saw what was happening there and made some good contacts. And as I came from a sales background we decided to see what would happen in business."

Sales were made initially through stalls at gay nights in clubs, and the welcome they received was sufficient to justify opening a store in 1984. They actually opened two stores on the same day, one in Manchester and one in London. "It was a major gamble for us," Paul told me. "There was still a stigma attached to being gay as well as going into a sex shop, so gay people had a double problem... We wondered if gay people would come out in the daytime shopping."

The new stores proved popular, but not with everyone: "We had a lot of harassment from the police," said Paul. "They tried to close us down by increasing the frequency of the raids, turning up with dozens of officers. They would take our stock and hang on to it for as long as they wanted."

Most people, if faced with the constant threat of prosecution and having their stock removed by the police, would probably look for an alternative way of making a living. But, as active members of the community they were serving, the directors felt they were on a mission which transcended mere commerce.

Eventually the authorities realised their efforts could be better spent elsewhere – though only after several prosecutions had failed – and Clonezone was allowed to go about its business, expanding into mail order, wholesale, publishing, and manufacturing.

It was far from being the only gay-focused business in the UK but, with its multi-channel routes to market, it was among the most visible, along with rival Millivres Prowler Group.

Millivres Prowler Group (MPG) first started trading in 1974. It too had endured years of police raids and prosecutions, but it was thriving when I visited the firm in 2004. Its stores were not only complemented by mail order, wholesale, publishing, and manufacturing divisions, it was even selling its products into 'straight' sex shops, though this could be an uphill task. Director of sales Nick Hilton told me: "We had a store in Birmingham say: 'We don't have any gay people here, there is no call for that sort of thing'. Retail can underestimate the pink pound. It is a well-known fact that gay men have high disposable incomes and enjoy a bit of a Peter Pan lifestyle. You often find a household with two good incomes coming in and fewer responsibilities, so they have more money to spend on entertainment."

Although Clonezone and MPG were competitors, they also co-operated for the greater good: "We have always worked closely with Clonezone," Nick told me. "For the past 30 years we have been lobbying for the rights of gay people and we actively support Stonewall, the equality lobbying group, so we are used to getting our hands dirty."

Their efforts, along with many others, have resulted in a far more inclusive society, where the initialism LGBTQIA+ (lesbian, gay, bisexual, trans, queer, intersex, asexual and more), along with the colours of the rainbow flag, are now firmly entrenched in mainstream culture, and gay products can be found anywhere sex toys are sold.

An interesting recent trend has been the move away from gender-specific products to gender-neutral ones. While this is a response to our increasingly non-binary society, there are also sound financial reasons behind it: why exclude a large part of your potential market by targeting just one 'type'?

A range called Gender X was launched in 2022, which featured toys in neutral colours with no obvious target market identified on the rather plain white boxes, but the first 'one size fits all' – if you'll excuse the expression – sex toy that was marketed to everyone was The Cone.

Unlike the majority of sex toys on the market at the time of its launch in June 2006, The Cone was quite substantial in size, but it also looked friendly and approachable. Its round conical shape had a diameter of 185 mm and a height of 115 mm, and its internal gubbins was protected by soft pink silicone.

After inventor Alan Driscoll designed a wooden S&M chair, he went on to make one out of silicone with a vibrator inside, and The Cone was a development of this. A true hands-free product, it weighed a hefty 375g and utilised a pokey 3,000 rpm motor.

It was the debut release by Twisted Products and not long after launch MD Sara Parkinson told me: "The Cone is non-threatening so it is a good introduction to the world of sex toys as well as being fun for the seasoned enthusiast. We've had a few hetero males testing the product too; one called it 'two-second Viagra'. We hope the gay market will welcome this toy as much as the hetero market. We have had a number of gay testers and they loved it – we are still missing a number of prototypes..."

It also appealed to Jonathan Ross, who featured it on his show, but there was more to The Cone than just a quick thrill, as Sara explained: "Being non-sexual in appearance is a real plus. I have one on my coffee table at home and no-one has a clue what it is until I tell them. Because it's only moderately penetrative, our testers found that it seems to tighten the area in which it was being used. We are looking into the benefits of this in muscle rehabilitation for post-pregnancy and incontinence sufferers with possible benefits for anti-natal use too. Our testers noticed an increase in libido and sensitivity too."

Its £49.99 retail price did not deter buyers and The Cone appeared to be a success, with international distribution agreements signed and ambitious plans to develop the concept further. Sadly that didn't happen. If you google 'The Cone sex toy' now, all that remains are positive reviews and the impression that a pristine example is now a collector's item.

Rather surprisingly, no one has attempted to fill the Cone-shaped gap by creating a similar toy to the original, though in 2014 PicoBong made the bold claim that its Transformer was the world's first 'truly inclusive' sex toy.

The company added that the product transcended the labels normally ascribed to sexuality and gender and, to be fair, it was something different: imagine a short (60cm) skipping rope made of silicone, where both 'handles' vibrate. Now imagine the 'rope' is flexible but stiff and will hold any shape it is twisted into. "This versatility allows it to be used by anyone – male, female, trans, cis – of any sexuality in any way they want," the company enthused. "It's a rabbit vibe, a clitoral massager, a cock ring, a G-spot vibe, a prostate massager and a million other things. It can be wrapped around furniture and around body parts – any way you wish. It is, quite simply, as twisted as the user's imagination."

Ronja Moln, PicoBong UK account manager, added: "Never before has anyone created a toy for everyone. The Transformer aims to awaken sexual exploration and make people realise they don't need to be confined by the labels placed on them."

Inclusivity does not just mean widening a product's focus, it can also mean narrowing it. Buck-Off, which was released in 2016, was said to be the world's first adult toy designed for the trans male community.

It was created by Perfect Fit in collaboration with adult-entertainment star and activist Buck Angel, who commented at the time: "I am so thrilled to finally be releasing an adult toy specific to the trans male community. I believe sex is a big part of the transition process and finding and exploring your new body can be challenging. This is something I have been working on for years, and Steve (Callow, Perfect Fit CEO) saw this as an important product, not only for the pleasure products world, but also because it acknowledges that transmen are valued enough to have their own adult toy."

2021 saw the launch of Exo, a wearable device 'powered' by the user's own natural body movements, which was inspired by the trans female community. It was unlike anything else on the market though I thought it shared some characteristics of the original Rock Chick from 2003, which dished out rewards to the user in direct proportion to the physical effort put in.

"That's a fair comparison, at least with regard to the design goal of a device that stimulates the user in a self-contained, body-powered way," Exo founder Lucas Hartmann acknowledged. "It is important to note that one of the key challenges for Exo was creating something that could adapt to a wide range of body morphology. This problem requires that you solve for variation in height, waist, adipose tissue, erect length and erect diameter, all while providing a stimulation experience that's roughly similar for as many users as possible. Some of the one-size-fits-all toys may miss this and leave users feeling like toys aren't designed for them. While Exo does still have some size limitations, the goal is that it can accommodate a wide range of body types and sizes."

Lucas, a self-described 'non-binary mechanical engineer', said: "I was seeing trans women having sex and they seemed to be really enjoying being in the moment, but then they'd have to stop, change position and masturbate in order to climax. It seemed like there might be a way to create something that would allow them to stimulate themselves in the moment, and in fact, have the actual body movements they were already making help to drive that stimulation."

Users were required to simply adjust Exo's straps to their waist size, then connect the sleeve using two adjustable rings – practically any size penis could be accommodated – and lube up. "To our knowledge, there's no other masturbation sleeve, or sex toy of any kind really, that works the way that Exo does," said Lucas.

Also unveiled in 2021 and deserving a mention was VDOM. A prosthetic penis that was controlled by an app, it seemed ideal for the FTM trans community, sufferers of erectile dysfunction (ED), and anyone else seeking a 'working' penis.

VDOM was developed by US entrepreneur Glenise Kinard-Moore, who felt that existing products on the market had too many shortcomings. "To put it bluntly, I love sex and I wanted to be able to have sex with my wife anywhere, at any time, and just as easily as heterosexual couples can without any awkwardness," Glenise told *ETO*.

"The VDOM is by far the most challenging idea that I've worked on. But I felt like it had to be done for many reasons. There are many people who experience certain physical sexual restrictions – including ED and paraplegia – but only a very small handful of solutions that even to try to address those issues. I wanted to use my tech skills and knowledge to challenge myself to find a solution. I knew the prosthetic needed to be comfortable to wear all day, it needed to be hands-free as much as naturally possible, and it needed to be able to go from non-erect to erect via a simple process. We've achieved that, and as a result our customers are going to be able to ditch the strap-on."

Hot Octopuss has always been big on inclusivity and the firm revamped its website in 2019 to reflect this. The site included a 'non-binary button' that gave users the option to remove all gendered terminology plus it included sections devoted to those with disabilities, health issues, sexual concerns, older consumers, and trans and non-binary users. CEO Adam Lewis explained: "We were contacted by some trans and non-binary reviewers who said our gendered approach to marketing products excluded them. As a result, we reviewed both our mission and our approach to production and marketing."

In September 2021 Hot Octopuss became the first sex toy brand to exhibit at Naidex, which describes itself as 'Europe's most established event for supporting independent living, showcasing wide-ranging solutions to improve mobility and accessibility' within the disabled community.

This initiative was part of Hot Octopuss's disability and inclusion strategy, spearheaded by creative director Kelly Gordon, who said: "There are more than 20 million people living with disabilities in the UK alone. Yet, when it comes to sex, there is a massive supply gap when it comes to effective products, advice, and information for disabled people. [Exhibiting at] Naidex sends a powerful and progressive message to the disabled community that sex is for us and shouldn't be something that disabled people can't pursue or shouldn't want."

Rather surprisingly, considering how human beings are – on the whole – getting larger, it took until 2014 for a manufacturer to release a plus-size collection. US brand Sportsheets unveiled its Sportsheets Plus collection of sex toys, positioning tools, and strap-ons in sizes ranging from 12 to 30. The items featured longer straps, longer and wider pads, and more adjustability than the firm's standard lines.

The company said that with more than 55% of women purchasing clothing sized 16 or larger and 62% identifying as being overweight, it was essential for retailers to provide sexy, sensual options for every body type and recognise that healthy, satisfying sex had no bounds: "More women not only identify themselves as plus-size, but also embrace it with open minds and hearts," said Sportsheets president Julie Stewart. "While society still maintains a negative attitude toward larger women, with fat-shaming and other negative stereotypes, there's a resurgence of sex-positive celebrations of body image among women of all sizes and shapes. And these are the confident and sexually curious consumers that Sportsheets Plus speaks to."

Anyone starting a new business selling sex toys online needs a point of difference. They always did, but this was especially true in 2020 when newcomers were not only competing with the biggest names in the industry but also with the biggest name in any industry: Amazon.

Abs and Mac, the wife and husband duo behind Black Honey Toys, chose to specialise in sex toys and other pleasure enhancing products which reflected different shades of the Black skin. The BHT website stated: 'In an industry dominated by mainstream Eurocentric standards of beauty, we want to create a space where shoppers feel empowered and represented. We provide shoppers with a carefully selected inventory which reflects Black sexuality and skin tones. We are championing the idea that online sex toy shops should be more racially inclusive in their store displays and product range.'

When I interviewed the founders of Black Honey Toys in March 2021, the firm had only been trading for just over a year, and although most of that year was dominated by a pandemic, Abs described the response to the business as "incredible" and "pleasantly surprising". She went on to say: "The response we've received reaffirms our belief in what we are trying to achieve with BHT – to champion diversity and inclusivity within the online sex toy retail space."

Abs and Mac's professional backgrounds were in media intelligence and project management, and they had no previous experience of the pleasure sector: "That comes with obvious disadvantages as we do not have the contacts and the background knowledge," Abs said. "However, the flip side to this is that we come into the industry with a healthy dose of curiosity and the ability to confront challenges with fresh eyes rather than with rules of thumb."

I credit a lot of the progress made towards inclusivity to the women who have chosen to make their careers in the sex toy sector. There have always been smart, business-savvy women in the industry – three of the best-known pioneers from the last century were Ky Hoyle of Sh!, who was mentioned in chapter seven, Susan Colvin, the founder and CEO of US manufacturer CalExotics, and Jacqueline Gold of Ann Summers – but now there are many.

As companies expanded through the noughties, women were frequently recruited to sales and PR positions. And while some found the environment less than comfortable, the ones who stayed often saw their responsibilities, positions, and salaries, grow in direct proportion to their employers' fortunes – as did their influence. Some are still in the industry, while others have used it as a stepping stone to positions at household-name brands – and that in itself is a pretty good indicator of how mainstream the sex toy sector is becoming.

As mentioned earlier, it is also now commonplace for new sex toy start-ups to be headed by women. They frequently bring expertise from other areas into the industry and rather than starting from a kitchen table or garage, like many of their predecessors, they come armed with ambitious business plans and funding.

Start-ups – whoever they are headed by – usually fall into two camps: those with a bright idea to plug a perceived gap in the market, or those who see the sector as ripe for exploiting. Sadly I have encountered several of the latter who seem to look down on the industry they are entering. It could be the PR agencies they hire to write their press releases, admittedly, but I have lost count of how many 'sex-positive' newbies claim to be on a mission to 'destigmatise' sex toys.

Presumably the activities of all the firms mentioned in this book completely passed them by. It was even more irritating to read such guff from start-ups who had just slapped their cool branding on seen-it-all-before generic toys.

Alongside inclusivity, the sex toy sector has also embraced sustainability in recent years. 'May your vibrators be strong, and your batteries be plentiful' may once have been an apt blessing to wish on a friend but all the best sex toys are mains powered or USB rechargeable now, with battery-operated models tending to be either entry level (basic), built to a price (cheap), or a classic design (ancient).

Manufacturers have also experimented with 'alternative' energy sources too: while wind and wave are obviously rather impractical, CalExotics unveiled a solar powered vibrating bullet as long ago as 2004. Solar Sensations came with a power pack that could even be charged via exposure to artificial light, and when full it could run the accompanying bullet for 55 minutes at high speed.

Rather astonishingly, this bright idea was never copied by anyone else, even though the technology wasn't exactly cutting edge in 2004 (I had a very similar device for my Game Boy Advance SP almost a decade earlier). Admittedly the solar panel required eight hours of exposure to bank that 55 minutes of vibrating power, but I'm sure the tech must have moved on during the last two decades. Incidentally, if you fancy getting hold of a Solar Sensations, there was a brand-new unused one on eBay with a $14.99 Buy It Now price while I was writing this passage.

Anyone who couldn't wait eight hours for their vibe to charge, but whose eco principals prohibited them from using a battery-operated model, would have rejoiced at the launch of Earth Angel in 2009. Remember the wind-up radio invented by Trevor Baylis? Earth Angel used the same principal: a key in the vibe's base could be unfolded and used to crank the internal motor. Four minutes of winding generated enough power for 30 minutes of vibrations, and any unused energy was stored for next time.

It was created by Irish company Caden Enterprises and it was even made from recyclable parts and delivered in 100% recyclable packaging. "Our mission is to reduce the amount of waste batteries that make their way to landfills around the world while also making toys that cost the consumer less to purchase and maintain," said a spokesperson for Caden Enterprises at the time of launch. "Over the last few years there have been attempts made to produce a 100% environmentally friendly sex toy but none have so far lived up to expectations. 'Green' sex toy manufacturers are focusing more on the materials used in their toys than the operation of the toys."

I expected Earth Angel to be a huge success – how could it not be? – but the following year Caden Enterprises announced it was leaving the adult industry in order to pursue other markets, and it offered to either licence or sell its patented technology to other sex toy firms. I can only assume a well-known battery manufacturer surreptitiously snapped it up and buried it, because I never heard of it again.

The first eco-themed range of products was Leaf, which was created by Canadian firm BMS Factory in 2011. There were six models in the range, all quite small in size and sporting names such as Bloom, Fresh, Life, Spirit, Touch, and Vitality. Each vibe's design was influenced by an actual leaf and its functions controlled by just a single unobtrusive raised nubbin; holding it down cycled through the vibration options while pressing it quickly turned the Leaf on or off. Power came from a rechargeable lithium battery, and the seamless silicone construction of the vibes meant the whole surface area of the toy could be used.

Green in colour, as well as intentions, Leaf models came in brown cardboard packaging and contained paper from ethically harvested forestry initiatives. BMS CEO Steve Bannister told me at the time of its launch: "Leaf's main draw is that it is a lifestyle choice. When you invest in a Leaf product, you are investing in your pleasure, your sexual health, and the environment around you… Aside from a few necessary packaging elements, there really isn't anything that comes with Leaf that you need to dispose of."

US manufacturer Blush Novelties went further in 2016 with the launch of its Gaia range of biodegradable sex toys. Made from a bioplastic polymer compound mixed with corn starch, it was said to biodegrade within 90 days in a commercial composting facility.

It followed this with a tree-planting initiative to coincide with Earth Day: Blush pledged to plant one tree for every online or bricks and mortar store that shared a photo of Gaia products on its shelves.

The company also offered cash incentives to all employees who bought or leased electric cars or installed solar panels in their homes. "Climate change is a real issue," said Blush COO Eric Lee. "I want to do my best to protect the future of all children. I am hoping, with this initiative, that I can influence a few people in our small company, and by announcing this to our industry, I can influence other business owners to also do something similar. Together, as an industry, we can make a difference."

In 2022 the company announced it had developed a new 'natural and sustainable' material called BioTouch, which offered high tensile strength and long-lasting durability but was made from compostable plant-based material. Blush CEO Verna Meng said: "Knowing how sexual wellness products have grown to play such an important role in a healthy lifestyle, we wanted to develop products that can make a difference beyond the bedroom, but also in our beautiful environment."

An honourable mention should also go to Womanizer. As detailed in chapter eleven, it launched a crowdfunding campaign with a difference in 2021 to promote its Premium Eco model and the same year saw UK start-up Love Not War launch its debut toy collection. Called Koi, it was made from predominantly recycled and recyclable materials. Its green credentials were further boosted by the use of eco-friendly glue, soy ink, and cardboard packaging. Most importantly, all models in the Love Not War range shared a common base – so users could purchase a different 'head' if they fancied a change.

"We have watched consumers become increasingly concerned about the Earth in recent years," said Love Not War CEO Will Ranscombe. "Gen Z, also dubbed the green generation, are increasingly making changes to their daily lives in order to be more sustainable."

Ranscombe added that while this was being reflected in the mainstream, he thought the pleasure products sector had been slow to address consumers' needs for sustainability: "We believe that consumers are actively looking for products and services that use recycled materials and if manufacturers are going to choose to ignore said trends then they need to be prepared to be left behind," he warned.

In 2022 Love Not War released Maya, which was made from 99% recycled aluminium and also compatible with all the company's heads. Described as the firm's most sustainable product so far, Love Not War promised to plant a tree through global reforestation charity One Tree Planted for every Maya purchased.

Also in 2022, US manufacturer Doc Johnson was doing its bit for sustainability by recycling dildos into footwear. The Plastic Sole initiative, in collaboration with LA-based shoe brand Rose In Good Faith, saw unused and discarded Doc Johnson dildos recycled into millimetre-sized cubes which were then mixed with non-bleach EVA (Ethylene-Vinyl Acetate) foam and injection moulded into the shape of a shoe. The resulting Plastic Sole had a retail price of $130.

Taking inclusivity and sustainability seriously are clear indicators that the sex toy sector is maturing, but so too are acquisitions, high-profile mergers, and the arrival of venture capitalists.

Acquisitions were nothing new, and usually involved big players snapping up the assets of smaller concerns, perhaps because the owners wanted a change of career or were finding business a bit of a slog.

There had never been any major industry mergers, but that changed in 2018 when two of the big boys – Womanizer and Standard Innovation Corporation – got into bed together and woke up as the Wow Tech Group. Womanizer pioneered 'pleasure air technology' while Standard Innovation was the firm behind the We-Vibe range of products.

"The combined company brings together two of the industry's most successful, innovative, and recognised brands," said Womanizer managing director Johannes Plettenberg.

"Bringing together the teams behind these brands provides an exceptional foundation for a new phase of growth."

While the industry was still acclimatising to the news, an even bigger bombshell was dropped: Telemos Capital acquired a majority stake in Lovehoney. "We got to the stage last year when we could see turnover approaching £100m, and we thought, this has become a massive business and we owe it to the business and the staff to make the best of it," Lovehoney co-founder Richard Longhurst told me. "The skills and knowledge and expertise that Neal and I have have got us here but we might need more help to get us to the next stage. Can £100m become £200m and £300m? We think so, and we've now got the right people to help us do it."

Telemos Capital was formed the previous year by Philippe Jacobs, who was also co-chairman of Swiss investment firm Jacobs Holding AG, to invest in consumer, healthcare, and business-services companies: "This is a mainstream business catering to the needs of couples with a female-friendly approach," he said in a statement. "There is a huge momentum behind ecommerce in general but because of the discretion and anonymity behind retailing this product it is suited to growth."

The times they were a-changin', and in 2019 the two founders stepped down from the day-to-day running of Lovehoney and ex-Sainsbury's and Heineken marketing director Sarah Warby was appointed CEO.

I sat down with Sarah at her first trade show, when she had only been in the role for four weeks, and she told me: "This is an exciting progressive business that is performing really well and what it does, at its heart, is make people happy. Who wouldn't want to be a part of that?"

This was not long after it emerged that high street chain Boots would be stocking Lovehoney products online and in some of its stores, and Sarah explained: "The Boots deal is really exciting. It's early days but it's a fairly intelligent way to dip our toes in the water and see what happens."

At the very least, I pointed out, it would give the Lovehoney brand massive mainstream exposure, and Sarah agreed: "For customers, brands are a beacon," she said. "The consumer knows what to expect, they are something to rely on. It's very rare that you have industries where brands don't have that role and the Lovehoney brand does that for our customers. I come from Sainsbury's where roughly half of what is sold is made by branded manufacturers and half is made by Sainsbury's. The Sainsbury's brand is just as strong in its food ranges as it is as a big sign over the door. Customers know what they are going to get."

Wow Tech Group was back in the headlines in March 2020, when global private equity group CDH Investments acquired a 'significant stake' in the firm. CDH said it believed strongly in the long-term prospects of the global sexual wellness industry and intended to invest significant resources into Wow Tech's innovation and marketing activities to further grow the business.

MD Thomas Lanyi said: "We identified the tremendous potential of the industry and had been actively searching for a high-quality, professionally managed company to commit our capital and expertise to. During the course of last year's discussions, we developed strong confidence in the management, products, and business model of the Wow Tech organisation. CDH will strongly support the continuation of the current business platform and add significant resources to empower the management team around CEO Johannes von Plettenberg to accelerate the global expansion of the company, organically and through acquisitions."

The deals kept coming: in January 2021 the EQOM Group was created when two European suppliers – Eropartner Distribution and EDC Retail – merged. Although both firms were based in the Netherlands, they each had customers throughout Europe, including the UK, and joining forces would result in them complementing and strengthening each other as well as increasing their purchasing power.

If the EQOM deal had been a bit of a surprise, jaws positively dropped in August 2021 when Lovehoney merged with Wow Tech Group to form the industry's first 'supergroup'. Lovehoney had acquired Swiss brand Amorama the previous year, and Johannes Plettenberg, CEO of the newly named Lovehoney Group commented: "We are excited about this transaction and partnership. Amorana, Lovehoney, and Wow Tech share the same mission to destigmatise sexuality, empower people to enjoy a fulfilling love life, and experience sexual happiness. Combined, we will be even better placed to contribute to bringing sexual happiness to the centre of society."

The new supergroup could boast more than 730 staff, located in ten offices around the world. On the day the merger was announced it made global headlines, and not just on B2B websites. *The Wall Street Journal* brought the story to many people's attention, while others found out about it from sources as diverse as *Forbes*, *The Telegraph*, *Private Equity News*, *Global Cosmetics News*, and a whole host of others.

The deal was said to be worth an astonishing $1.2 billion and the new supergroup was expected to generate sales of more than $400m in its first year – about double the combined 2020 level – making it the world's largest sexual wellness company measured by revenue.

The industry's first supergroup was joined by the industry's second supergroup in September 2021 when EQOM Group acquired two European retail businesses: the Norwegian Kondomeriet and the Dutch Christine Le Duc.

In a statement announcing the new initiative, EQOM Group said: "The acquisition of these two major retail brands creates a partnership between Europe's biggest erotic companies with both a powerful online sales channel and physical stores."

The statement added that Kondomeriet was the largest supplier of sex toys in Norway, while Christine le Duc was the oldest erotic company in the Netherlands. The new acquisitions increased the EQOM Group head count to 300, and it had ambitious plans to increase its €100m 2020 turnover to over €500m over the next four years: "Not only do we want to keep our position as European market leader in 2025, but we also want to become a global player with a total turnover of half a billion euros," said group chairman Eric Idema. "The new consortium will enable us to continue to respond to the worldwide increasing interest in sexual wellness products such as sex toys."

Over the next few months, EQOM added two more European online retailers, Amorelie and Nytelse.no, to its portfolio, and further marking out 2021 as the year the industry went corporate was the launch of Amboy Street Ventures by Healthy Pleasure Group.

Described as the world's first venture capital fund focused on sexual health for all genders and women's health technology start-ups, Amboy Street Ventures took its name from the first US birth control clinic, which opened at 46 Amboy Street in New York in 1916, when prescribing and distributing information about birth control and contraception was illegal.

The fund's first two investments were in female-focused sexual wellness brand Dame Products and Gennev, the digital health platform for women in menopause, but the firm said it intended to cover all investment areas in the sexual and women's health industry across medtech, femtech, sextech, healthtech, telehealth and wellness.

Amboy Street Ventures was headed up by three female principals – Carli Sapir, Dominnique Karetsos, and Dr Maria Peraza Godoy – and Sapir said: "We believe billion-dollar companies will emerge in order to bridge the gap between the underserved sexual and women's healthtech space and the needs of today's society. We are female investors who are living through the issues facing women. We know the potential to help drive the market and make genuine change happen."

As we've seen, this is one sector not afraid of change. It's had quite the journey since the prime minister and the monarch of the day joined hands to welcome in the new millennium – and it's far from over.

Afterword

This book is based on my time with ETO, and its source material is the people, products, companies, and events that I encountered. Apologies to all who are not represented within its pages, particularly the pioneers who were active in the industry prior to the period covered by this book.

Also available by Dale Bradford: The Honey Peach Affair

A social drink with Britain's hottest adult entertainment star is the starting point for the biggest adventure of film reviewer Bruce Baker's life.

When her sister asks for his help in investigating the star's disappearance, law-abiding Bruce chalks up a charge sheet worthy of a career criminal, during his encounters with the unscrupulous and the fearsome – while dealing with a disagreeable boss who is looking for an excuse to sack him.

Sharing his journey is a virtuous anti-porn campaigner, whose cause Bruce inadvertently elevates to national prominence, and it culminates in Bruce sitting on one of the biggest stories any journalist could ever hope to uncover.

But he doesn't want to write it.

A murder mystery set in the adult industry of 2003, The Honey Peach Affair is available in paperback and ebook formats from Amazon platforms worldwide.

Printed in Great Britain
by Amazon

18341677R00098